LIVE
THE
LIFE

Minister Bill

WESTBOW
PRESS®
A DIVISION OF THOMAS NELSON
& ZONDERVAN

WestBow Press books may be ordered through booksellers or by contacting:

WestBow Press
A Division of Thomas Nelson & Zondervan
1663 Liberty Drive
Bloomington, IN 47403
www.westbowpress.com
1 (866) 928-1240

ISBN: 978-1-9736-1737-2 (sc)
ISBN: 978-1-9736-1736-5 (e)

Print information available on the last page.

WestBow Press rev. date: 01/26/2018

Live The Life

It's time to start living the life you sing about in your song. It's time to wake up in the morning feeling good about yourself because you know that you are a child of God. Knowing that nothing can keep you down for long because Jesus is walking with you every step of the way. You don't have to face trouble alone. You are on top of the world because Jesus is by your side. We all have troubles. Jesus told us that we will have troubles in this life. It's time to start telling our troubles how big our God is. It's time to start praying for that person who has been giving you a hard time. Praying that soon she/he will find Jesus and the Holy Spirit will take control of their life. It's time to start thanking God for His many blessings. So many that you can't count them all. It's time to smile knowing that the best is yet to come. Knowing that all of life's experiences are only temporary. You are going to make it because God wants you to make it. All you have to do is BELIEVE.

THIS BOOK IS DEDICATED TO THE ONE I
LOVE
ETHEL LEE GRIFFIE ROBERTS

MOTHER

About The Author

Minister Bill has been a member of a Missionary Baptist Church for more than sixty-five years. He served in numerous capacities in an effort to help the church better serve the Kingdom of God. He served in the youth ministry, transportation ministry, business manager and treasurer, and for more than twelve years in the deacon's ministry. He was ordained as a Minister of the Gospel by the National Organization of Ministers in the year 2015. He is the author of the book entitled "Between The Lines" as well as this book "Live The Life". He often states that he is just a nobody trying to tell everybody about the Saving Power of Jesus Christ. Two of his favorite sayings are (You make me smile with my heart) and (Can you imagine how much I love you). The degree of joy given him can only come from God. The love that he has for God takes a very strong imagination. Minister Bill believes the primary purpose of religion is to help people live life more abundantly by forming a loving relationship with our Heavenly Father through Jesus Christ.

Live The Life

We tell the world that we love our Heavenly Father. We attend prayer and praise services, bible study, Sunday school, church services. We sing pretty songs of praise. Animism. The belief in the existence of spirit or soul, as distinct from matter. Then we return to our lives of anxiety. Disturbance in mind regarding some uncertain event, misgiving, worry. Fear and apprehension regarding the future. The way we live our lives is evidence of our faith. That building we go to on Sunday morning is not the church. The people in it are the church. The church does not exist only for it's members. The purpose of the church is to serve the community through the power of the Holy Spirit. The people of the church must serve the community. They, however, cannot serve others until they understand their own purpose for living. They cannot serve others until they accept the Lord into their lives seven days a week not just on Sunday. When they are in their houses not just the House of God. God must control our minds each day of our lives. Only through the Spirit of God can we over power the anxiety of life. Once we accept His promise to live, protect, and provide a place for us with Him for eternity, then only will we live our lives with peace and without anxiety. We will Live The Life we sing about in our songs.

Live The Life

LIVE THE LIFE God wants you to live. Live the life you sing about in your song. You are here by the Grace of God. He has made life mentally comfortable when you understand His purpose. It is all in the mind. Live this life in a way that shows the world you have the Victory given to you by Jesus. You don't have to worry. He won't let you down. Know each day that Jesus is with you. He helps you control your highs and lows. You can experience Joy knowing that in this life what goes up must come down. You learn to be content knowing that this too shall pass. Knowing that nothing can be out of control when God is in control. Believing that nothing can prosper against you because your God is with you.

INSPIRATION

YOU are a WINNER!

LIVE THE LIFE

By:
The Author of (Between The Lines)

Minister Bill

A Better Understanding Of God's Message

A BETTER UNDERSTANDING OF GOD'S MESSAGE

Heaven, Eternity, Paradise. We are told that it is beyond human imagination. No wonder it is so difficult to get to. Only by the Grace of God. God must have standards by which He determines who He will grant His Grace. We are told that our good works will have no effect upon our Salvation. We must ask ourselves do we serve a God of justice? Did He give us all of those instructions as to what to do and not to do for nothing? Is it that He will not use them when passing His judgment? God knows your heart. That will be His first consideration. That is not enough. He will put you through test after test to find out if you are for real. He is THE all-powerful God. Why do you think He permits Satan and his temptations to remain effective? The primary test that you will witness is life. The way you live your life, your success in fighting Satan's temptations, will be given great consideration come judgment day.

This book was written for the purpose of helping you to gain a better understanding of God's message. The knowledge of the secrets of the kingdom of heaven is our purpose. Too many see and hear but do not understand. You will read some things you will never hear in church. The author is not limited by organizational standards. There are some things that your pastor believes that he will not tell you. You will read some things you will never read in the bible. To really understand God's message, you must read more than the bible. God blessed you with a limited amount of time to get it right. To show Him that you are for REAL. His determinations are made before He calls your number. Tomorrow was meant for some, but, tomorrow may never come.

Understanding The Power Of God

Understanding The Power Of God

There are people who have been in the church for numerous years who do not understand the power of God. A person makes the statement that he would like to believe God controls all. A deacon hears this remark and laughs. This same deacon tells the people in attendance that if they do not believe every word of the bible, they might as well close the bible and go home. Here is a deacon in a Baptist church who does not have an understanding of the power of God. Toddlers have been shot down in their homes. 12 year olds have been gun down in our parks. People are being gun down in church and college. Yet, there are people who will tell you that God controls everything that happens. Satan and his temptations. Why is it that God permits him to be effective? God is all-powerful. He could destroy Satan with nothing more than a word. That is not the way God uses His power. God has unlimited power, however, He will use power in ways we are not meant to understand. God does not control everything that happens in this world. He could. He has the power to do so. God has His own agenda. He has told us that our ways are not His ways. Stop trying to figure out God. That's not the reason you were put here. You were put here to worship, serve, honor, praise, and give Him the Glory. You were not put here to understand how He rules this world. Jesus did not know everything. He was asked when He would return. His statement was, only the Heavenly Father knows. No one, not even Jesus, knows all about God. That's where your trust is tested. When you see the world seemingly falling apart around you, can you, will you, trust in the Lord? One of the reasons God permits us a limited number of years to live could be because He is telling us that He is the boss. You can't get bigger than God. You can be the most powerful person on earth, but, you will never be the most powerful in the world. We Christians want it that way. Yes, we fear His judgment. Our primary reason is because we love Him. He first loved us. He still loves us. He will always love us. Nothing can separate us from the love of God. He is our fortress in whom we will always trust. Praise His Holy Name.

Worthy

Life can be complicated. We have to deal with many different considerations at the same time. Realism, emotion, believes. Addiction goes beyond our physical state. We become addicted to a way of thinking. This is what I believe and everything else is wrong. Some believe God made the bible perfect. Some believe we should believe every word just as written or close the bible and go home. Because you believe it does not make it right. More human beings than can be counted have been involved in composing the bible. None of them were perfect, therefore, the bible could not be perfect. There is only one perfect entity that has ever influenced this earth and that is God. Through Him we have been given Jesus and the Holy Spirit. Nothing else is perfect. We are to learn by listening first and by reading second. When listening, we must use our minds to control realism, emotions and belief. Maybe I'm wrong. Maybe there is no God. Maybe Jesus is not the Son of God. Maybe there is no Holy Spirit. But using all that I have to work with, I don't think so. I believe because I chose to believe. I want there to be a God. I want Jesus to be the Son of God. I want there to be Salvation. I want to spend eternity with God in Paradise. I want there to be a perfect God.

He is worthy to be praised. You are not Jesus. You were not even born perfect. Scripture reads of a person who looks at himself or herself in the mirror then walks away and immediately forgets what he or she looks like. This does not take into account people who want to forget what they see in the mirror. Some want to forget what they look like. They know that they are not all they should be. They think I have so many problems. I drink too much. I have a temper. I have an addiction. Man, if I could start all over again. If I only knew then what I know now. I want to make God a part of my life, but, with all of these problems, I'm not worthy. Maybe after I straighten myself out. These are people who do not understand God's message. It's not about you. You were made that way so that you will have to depend upon the Lord if you are ever going to find peace. You were born a sinner because God wants you to depend on Him. You will never be worthy enough to come to God. He loves you just the way you are. He will help you through your troubles if you ask Him for help. You don't have to live this life alone.

He sent Jesus to show you the way. It's not about you. It's about Jesus. His coming His presents His passing. God will do for you just what He did for Jesus if you let Him. Right to the Resurrection. Eternity. Paradise. You have to only praise God, follow Jesus, help God's children. Ask Him for His help. Ask and it shall be given. Seek and you will find. Knock and the door will be open unto you.

I Must Be About My Father's Business

On your tomb stone will be your name, your date of birth and your date of death. Is that all you will be remembered for? What happen in-between? Will your name be written in the Book of Life? Some have accumulated millions, but, they will leave here with exactly the same thing you will leave here with, nothing. You had nothing when you came into this world. You will have nothing when you leave. Some were slapped on the butt at birth to force crying. Some have continued to be slapped on the butt and have never stopped crying. Life is filled with problems troubles. Many cannot be avoided. If we are not coming out of a storm, we are going into one. The quality of life will be determined by how you deal with problems. One thing is for sure. Trouble don't last always. Sooner or later trouble will end, while you live or when you die. When you entered this life you didn't have any troubles. After you leave this life, you will not have any troubles.

Why are some people remembered far after death while others are almost forgotten immediately after the funeral? It's all about what you leave behind. You can leave a building with your name carved in stone. But sooner or later it will fall. You can leave a lot of money. Sooner or later it will all be spent. You can leave something much more valuable. Something that every person who has or will ever live will need. The Good News of God's love through our beloved Savior Christ Jesus. There can be no true happiness in life without peace. Peace within. The peace that can only be gotten through a true loving relationship with Jesus. This peace that will be passed along from generation to generation.

You will never be forgotten. They may not remember your name, but, you will never be forgotten. Your actions will live forever in the hearts of generation after generation. To God be the Glory for the things you have done.

The Mystery Of The Holy Ghost

Words and terms that can be the same yet different. In the King James version of the bible, we find the term Holy Ghost used 97 times and the term Holy Spirit only stated 7 times. Yet, in later versions of the bible, the term Holy Ghost is almost eliminated and replaced with Holy Spirit. People do not like the term Ghost. It makes one think of death and that is the last thing we want to think about. Many believe the two terms to be the same. Some believe they are the same, but, there is a difference. They believe the Holy Ghost will be sent by God to one place at one time whereas the Holy Spirit can be in numerous places at the same time. A person's dad had been sick a long time, yet, he was up and around. This day was no different from any other. That night while sleep he saw his dad dying. He later was told that it happened exactly the way he saw it in his dream at exactly the same time. He believed that this was a message from the Holy Ghost sent to him alone.

The mystery of the Holy Ghost. It is beyond human realization. But many of us know that it does exist. People do things suddenly that they never had the capacity to do before. People see and envision things that is beyond their understanding. Only by the power of God. He has done great things. We must accept and praise them not ever try to understand them. The way God works in our lives is a mystery not meant to be understood. Only meant to be accepted and appreciated.

This tells us that He is here. Through all our trials and tribulations, we don't have to worry. He won't let us down. We have learned to dance in the rain because we know God loves us and will, regardless of what happens in this life, take care of us. It feels good to be Saved. To have some understanding of what the future holds. We do believe that there will be a future after this life. A home in Paradise with the One we love.

Forgiveness

Forgiveness

"But go, tell the disciples and Peter, 'He is going ahead of you to Galilee. There you will see Him, just as He told you." (Mark 16:7). Why (and Peter)? Peter denied Jesus three times. Jesus asked Simon Peter three times, do you love me? Jesus understood that Peter was weak because he was human. Jesus forgave Peter. Jesus forgave Paul who tried to destroy the movement of Jesus. You are not Jesus. One of the major differences between Jesus and us is not the willingness but the capacity to forgive. People have done some bad things to us during our lives. Some of these people are evil. They enjoy hurting others. Some are misguided. They have limited capacity to think and reason. Some to whom you have done nothing harmful. Some to whom you have even done much to help. Both have one thing in common. They are thinking about everything but God.

You want to forgive them so you think I will forgive him this time, but, if he ever needs help, I will not lift a finger to help him. Or, I will forgive her this time, but, I will never speak to her again. I recall the story of a man whose son was killed by another youth. He forgave the boy who killed his son. He often went to prison to visit him, taking the Holy Spirit with him. Upon his release, he took him into his home. He took the person who killed his son into his home. Christlike forgiveness. Growing in the Spirit of God. Christianity is a journey. Ask God have you grown enough in His Spirit to sincerely forgive a person who has seriously hurt you. We believe we are Saved. But, we are not all we should be. We need God's help to become the people He wants us to be. We need God's help in our efforts to become more and more like Jesus every day.

Belief

Belief

Belief is a powerful word. It can lead you to war or great height. God promised the children of Israel the land of milk and honey. The problem was that another people already occupied the land. How would you feel if a person came into your home and told you to get out because the Lord had given your house to them? You would be very upset to say the least. You would be ready to fight. Christianity is not understood the same by all. Some believe the bible to be word perfect. No one can prove them wrong. Others believe that it is not word perfect because it was written and composed by numerous people none of whom were perfect. The Gospels of Matthew and Mark stated that while on the Cross Jesus said "Eloi, Eloi, lama sabachthani" (Mark 15:34) which means My God, My God why have You forsaken me. In the Gospels of Luke and John we do not find this quote. Luke states that Jesus said "Father, into your hands I commit my spirit". (Luke 23:46). John states "It is finished" (John 19:30). Belief. Who do you believe? Mark was the first Gospel written. It is not known if Mark ever knew Jesus. Mark got much of his information from Peter. Peter disowned Jesus three times. He was in too much sorrow to be present at His death. Therefore, Peter could have only received his information from a third source. Mark's information came from second and third sources. It is believed that Matthew copied much of his Gospel from Mark. Therefore, if one was not completely correct, the other is not completely correct. John was there at the Cross. He could hear everything said by Jesus. He did not state that Jesus lost Faith in His Father.

Belief. Who do you believe? Do you actually believe that the human elements of the Son of God could ever over power His Spiritual elements even in the most painful moments of the death of Jesus? Do you actually believe that Jesus could ever think much less state that He believed His Father had forsaken Him? If you do, is your faith in the holiness of Jesus all that it should be?

No, the bible is not perfect. Good people with good intentions do not always get all of their facts straight. We have something perfect to believe in. God, Jesus, Holy Ghost. We cannot put the writings of man in an equal place. The bible is valuable. It is a source of Inspiration. Accept it for it's value.

Complete Faith

Complete Faith

I believe you will. Not, I believe you can. I don't have any doubts. I will leave it in your hands. There have been a few who have displayed complete faith. Abraham was willing to give up his son Isaac only because he had complete faith in God. How many of us would do the same? David was willing to fight a giant only because he had complete faith in God. Shadrach, Meshach and Abednego were willing to face death in a blazing fire furnace only because they had complete faith in God. There are people today who have that kind of faith. Complete Faith. They are in the minority. Most of us have shallow faith. There are different degrees of faith. Faith and love are not the same. Martha, the sister of Lazarus, loved Jesus but she did not have complete faith that He could put life back into her brother. Thomas loved Jesus, but, he did not have complete faith in His Resurrection. Mary Magdalene and Mary, the mother of Jesus, loved Him. They would not have gone to the tomb if they had complete faith in His words. They were told by the angel that He has risen. God freed the children of Israel from Egypt by performing numerous miracles. Seeing is not always believing. Even after these miracles, they rebelled against God. They did not have complete faith in their Heavenly Father.

Complete faith and forgiveness are two of the most difficult functions for a human being. God knows our weaknesses. He does not expect us to be perfect. We are not sinners because we sin. We sin because we are sinners. Is sin a measurement of faith? Is it safe to say that those with more faith sin less? It is easy to sin. Not doing that which you know you should do is a sin. When we sin, we can only seek God's forgiveness. Then try our best to do better and be smarter. If you are an alcoholic, stay away from bars. If you have a problem with drugs, stay away from pushers. If you are a homosexual, stay away from like people. God knows our weaknesses. We must also know them.

We want to please God because we love Him and fear His judgement. Without Faith it is impossible to please God. How deep is your faith? Be honest with yourself. We all have work to do.

Fight

I fought a good fight. I stayed the course. I kept the Faith. It would be wonderful if life was meant to be full of happiness. If you didn't have to find happiness because it would find you. We soon find out in life that each day is a fight just to continue to exist. We must do the same things over and over just to maintain our present status. If we have not prepared for old age, we are in even more trouble. We know that trouble don't last always. It will either end during this life or when we die. We have to mentally be able to handle it while we are alive. Why cut the grass? It is just doing to grow back anyway. Some people are not that strong. They try to find a way out through alcohol, drugs, or by hurting others. Sometimes we wonder why this race is so hard to run. Why the test when we try to do our best. People hurt us. People who we have done nothing to. People who we have done numerous things for yet they still show us an attitude. One thing is very important. We must not start acting like they are acting. This is part of the test. To show a good attitude toward those who show you a negative attitude. We soon learn that it was meant to be this way. All we can do is give it to Jesus and try to keep on keeping on.

Maybe it is because we have the wrong understanding of what life is all about. Why do we think it should be better for us than it was for Jesus? He was in trouble from birth. King Herod would have killed Him where it not for the protection of God moving Him from Bethlehem to Egypt. After His baptism, the devil tried three times to tempt Him to forsake His God. He had to fight off the temptations of Satan. The Pharisees and Sadducess wanted to kill Him. He had done nothing but good yet the chief priests hated Him. Pilate and Herod knew He was a good man, but, they were more interested in satisfying the people than do what was right.

If we have learned one thing from the life of Jesus, it is this life is nothing more than a test. God wants to know that you are for real. He could make everything in life a bed of milk and honey. He could destroy Satan and his temptations with only a word. He has prepared a place for us that is beyond imagination. He will only accept those who He knows are for real. Sometimes we have to go through problems to pass the test. Sometimes we feel that if we are not coming out of a storm we are going into one. It's all in the mind. Mental control is of great importance. Without it we are lost. Without it there is no way to win the fight. Keep your mind straight on Jesus. Only He can help you through it all. He can give you the mental control to dance in the rain. That's what life is about. Being able to dance in the rain. Knowing that there is something better on the other side of the river Jordan. I kept the Faith in God. That faith is our reason to stay on the battlefield for our Lord.

Messenger – Message

God has gone through many measures to let us know that He loves us and will always care for us. He wants us to know the level of His tolerance for both those who obey and disobey Him. He has sent numerous messengers to inform us of His Will and His Way. Samuel served God as a prophet, a priest and a military leader. Through God, He chose Israel's first two kings. Through God, He told them the Will of God. Through God, he let them know their sins before God. Isaiah was also a messenger of God. A prophet, poet, and politician. During the time of Isaiah, the people of Israel sinned greatly against God. They cared more about themselves than God and His Way. They harass the poor, went around drunk, cared about their outward appearance of religion but did little else. Like Samuel, Isaiah warned kings that military power or wealth or anything other than God would lead to disaster. Jeremiah was at first a reluctant messenger. He had many run ends with God. Many quarrels. But God offered no sympathy reminding him of His promise to stand by him. Like Samuel and Isaiah, Jeremiah gave top officials warnings they hated to hear. Samuel, Isaiah, and Jeremiah were God's messengers. They lived their lives with a sincere purpose of serving their Heavenly Father. They had no physical powers. They could only relate that told to them by the Almighty.

Then there was Jesus. He was not a messenger. He was the message. "The Word became flesh and made his dwelling among us." (John 1:14) God's Son, sent to do the work of the Father. God spoke in the only way we could truly understand, by becoming one of us. It was necessary to send Jesus because too often man would not listen to or believe God's prophets. Here we are over two thousand years later and there are still more people in this world who do not believe in Christ than do. They would not believe God's prophets and most still will not believe God's Son. All of His miracles, more than twenty-three as reported in Scripture. All of the times He controlled nature, more than eight as reported in Scripture. All the times He raised humans from the dead, more than three times as reported in Scripture. All the good that He has done for humankind. And they still will not believe.

God does not send anyone down below. People choose to go. The question has often been asked, will only those who believe in Jesus be Saved? I don't know the answer. I know what Jesus said, no one comes to the Father but by Me. I also know God's tolerance. Paul said He was forgiven for his ignorance and disbelief. Well, God will never have to forgive me for disbelief. Maybe ignorance, but, never for disbelief. I will trust in the Lord till I die.

What God Wants

What God Wants

From the moment we are born, it is all about what we want. As a kid, we want others to like and accept us. We want to be a part of something. We even think about our sexuality. Is this what I want to be? When we marry and have children, we think about what we want for them. We think about all the material things that we consider important. My kids have never been in a daycare. Their mother has always been there to take care of their every need because I worked long hard hours to make it happen. When we think about a career, we think only about ourselves. About money and making a living. 50% of people getting married don't stay that way very long. The most important entity in their lives is not the person they married. When you marry, you are making a commitment to do your best to make the life of your spouse happy. We assume we have all the answers. We never ask questions. Are you happy? What can I do to help make you better enjoy life? Maybe that person would rather eat a pizza with you than a steak alone. Drive a Ford Escort with you than a more expensive car without you. Your children need a hug. Even your teenage boy needs his dad to hug him. It stays with him more than words can express.

We think that nothing could be wrong with doing the best thing for the most people. How can we determine the best thing without first asking God? Believe it or not, evil makes a deeper impression on people than good. Take a good person who has been taught all the right things. Put that person on a daily base round people who do wrong and that person will start acting like those with whom he/she associates. We are not sinners because we sin, we sin because we are sinners. Sin is a part of our nature. God knows we are weak. We must also know our weaknesses. We go to church on a regular base because we know that we need spiritual reinforcement to stay on the right path. We read the same words in the bible over and over because we know that we need inspirational reinforcement. God knows that we need reinforcement. That is the reason He gave us the church and bible. God wants us to come to the conclusion that His Way is also our way. He wants you to give yourself to your family. This is much more important than material things. He wants you to share His message with others. If you hesitate to speak His name to others, don't expect Him to not take the same attitude toward you. He wants you to truly believe that there is nothing in this world more important to you than your Heavenly Father.

Why does it seem that society is not what it was? People are not what they use to be. There is a very simply answer. The family is not what it was. The teachings of God's Ways in the home is not what it once was. Separation from each other and from God. The family that prays together stays together.

Justice

Justice

Why is it so hard to live a life pleasing to God? All God wants is for us to do justice to Him, ourselves, and to others. Why is that so hard? He is the Creator of heaven and earth. The sky, trees, birds, animals, everything around us tells us that. It is paying Him justice by praising His name. The body you have been given is due respect in order to show Him gratitude. You pay Him justice by showing respect for the gift of God, your body. The second biggest sin of man is the manner in which he treats his follow man. Throughout history man has used force to make others do for him that which he should do for himself. It has always been that way. The bible tells us of the numerous times Israel was forced into slavery. If we read between the lines, we find that Israel held their own people as slaves. They approved of betting their slaves with rods. We know of the terrible treatment black people was subject to in the United States. We know of the holocaust Jews were subject to by the Germans. We don't have to go back 2000 years to see how badly human beings treat other human beings. It is happening as we speak. Murder, rape, drugs, alcohol abuse, human trafficking. Humans being treated worse than a decent person would treat an animal. This world deserves to be condemned. It is too bad that the few must suffer the crimes of so many. It will never stop. That is until God stops it. And He will.

God demands justice. God will not permit man's crimes against humanity forever. When we read between the lines, we understand that the bible, history, tells us exactly what will happen in the future. God does not want sacrifices or singing. He demands justice. God despises your religious feast. Stop just singing and do something to let justice roll on like a river, righteousness like a never-failing stream. Do something to give life back to that person who has been treated like anything other than a child of God. Do something.

We can continue to put on our fine clothes and go to church. Merchants can continue to pile up big profits. Enjoy the luxuries of life. Live in our new stone houses with our ivory-inland furniture. Enjoy top-grade meat and fine wine. Turn our backs on the oppression of the poor, dishonest business, bribery in court, privileges bought with money. Just remember, what goes up must come down.

They killed Jesus. They had more concern about themselves than God. One thing is for sure. God will have the last word.

A Conservative Christian

A conservative Christian is one who is incline to preserve the existing order of the Gospel. A non-conservative Christian is one who is incline to allow some adjustments to the changed conditions of today. A non-conservative Christian is one who thinks that they have the right to determine what is best for society. They believe that what is best for the majority of the people is the correct decision. Their primary problem is that they do not understand that no decision can be the right decision without obeying the Will of God.

God has told us thy shall not kill. He did not state thy shall not kill good people, but, it is all right to kill bad people. It is the responsibility of society to protect others from harm. If all the criminals who have been killed by the State where still alive, the responsibility to protect would have been accomplished. Some innocent people would not have been killed. It is the responsibility of society to make sacrifices to do that which is right. To physically support even the worse of society.

God has told us that it is a sin to have sex with another person of the same gender. He has made this so clear that it is impossible to think otherwise. Yet, there are people, who call themselves Christians, who believe that they should make adjustments to God's Will. They think that they know better than God. They think that God's Will should be adjusted to the changing conditions of today. They think that it is ok to support same sex marriages. They think that it is ok of just tell a homosexual we love you, but, never tell that person that they are committing a sin. They think it is ok to permit a homosexual to be the pastor of a church. We all are sinners. We ask God to forgive us and help us to correct our actions. How can a person who will not acknowledge his/her sins and ask for forgiveness and try to correct their actions lead others to Christ?

The word conservative and liberal, when it comes to Christianity, should be eliminated. There should be no such thing as a conservative or liberal Christian. There is only one kind of true Christian. One who believes in God's Word. One who will not conform to the ways of this world. A person who understands that God's Word rules yesterday, today, and tomorrow.

Re-Fuel

Re-Fuel

I'm Good! Have you ever heard a person make that statement after being asked how she/he is doing? That person is talking about his/her physical state. Life demands more. Life demands taking care of our mental and spiritual state as well. If you don't re-fuel your car, it will stop. If you don't re-fuel your body, it will stop. Everything needs nourishment to continue to function. Spirituality and our level of inspiration is no different. We have to deal with negative people every day. People who pass you while you are driving through an intersection. People who speak to you in a disrespectful manner. All we can do is try to stay away from them. If they push us too far, there is one saying that will start most of them thinking about themselves. (I thank God I don't act like you.) Don't say anything else. Just walk away. God will take care of business.

We have to have our spiritual tanks full to make it through some days. We have to wake up in the morning feeling good about ourselves. Good is a very important word. It is a requirement of God. He wants only the Good around Him. You can't go where He is unless Good is part of your character. It's not easy. It takes work. All good things take work and maintenance. You have to have respect for yourself and who you are. If you don't continually wash your body, you will smell bad. If you don't continually cut your grass, it will look bad. Keep it clean. If you don't continually re-fuel your spiritual and inspiration needs, you will act bad. We must use that which God has giving us if we are to keep it functional. Let a car sit without using it for two years and see what happens. Let a house sit for a long period of time without use and spider-webs will take over. We can stop spider-webs from covering our religious make-up by putting more logs on the fire. We re-fuel by reading the bible and other good spiritual writings. By going to church regularly. One of the biggest problems with Christians is that they do not use their gifts from God. Helping others physically and by spreading the Good News. Using our Christian gifts is extremely important.

Re-fuel. Wake-up in the morning feeling good that you are a good person. Believing that this world is nothing more than a stepping stone to God's paradise. 1.25 million people in this world die every day. This life is nothing more than a temporary assignment. Wake up with Jesus stayed on your mind. Feeling Good. Knowing that nothing can bring you down because Jesus has picked you up, turned you around and placed your feet on solid ground.

Examine Yourself

Examine Yourself

We have heard a thousand sermons and read thousands of words. We attend prayer and praise services, bible study, Sunday school, church services. We sing pretty songs of praise. It can only have meaning if we are growing in God's Spirit. That's what it's all about. Being better people, better Christians, this week than we were last week. God has told us to examine ourselves to determine if we are just going through the motions or if the Holy Spirit is truly within us and directing our lives.

Sometimes we must ask ourselves some trying questions to make this determination. Can we sincerely forgive a person who has seriously hurt us? Not, oh I will forgive him this time, but, if he ever needs help I will not lift a finger to help him. Not, I will forgive her this time, but, I will never speak to her again. No, we are talking about Christ-like forgiveness. A man's son was murdered by another youth. He forgave the murderer of his son. He often went to prison to visit him taking the Holy Spirit with him. Upon the release of the boy, the man took him into his home. He took the murderer of his son into his home. Christ-like forgiveness. Growing in the Spirit of God.

Have you grown in the Spirit enough to sincerely forgive a person who has seriously hurt you? We believe we are saved, but, we are not all we should be. We need God's help to become the people He wants us to be. We need God's help in our efforts to become more and more like Jesus every day.

Peter denied Jesus three times. After His Resurrection, Jesus told Mary to tell the disciples and 'Peter' were to meet Him. And Peter. Jesus wanted to be sure that Peter knew he was forgiven. It is reported that while on the Cross Jesus ask God to forgive those who were taking His life. Here is a man of God who is willing to forgive His murderers, yet, we have a problem with forgiving another while we are still alive.

People have done some awful things to other human beings. Things that only a sincere child of God could forgive. No one said the road would be easy. Stop just going through the motions. It can only have meaning if you are growing in God's Spirit. Examine yourself.

Opinion

Opinion

A conclusion or judgment held with confidence, but falling short of positive knowledge. That sounds like the definition of a belief. An opinion is often based on a belief. How many human beings have been executed wrongly because others believed wrong and stated their opinions based on their poor judgment? No two people have the same matrix of character. The character of a person can develop from many different sources. It can be inherited through genes from parents to child. It can be developed through learning both good and bad. A human being is a very complicated animal. The opinion of one can be an asset or very harmful to society.

Expressed with confidence, but falling short of positive knowledge. The sermon of a pastor stating that Jesus came to us for the purpose of gaining knowledge of human character fits this definition. Falling short of positive knowledge. God wanted to learn more about how a human being thinks and feels. To learn more about human emotions sorrow and happiness. We are talking about the Creator of mankind. The Creator who made mankind so complicated that mankind cannot figure him out. Yet, here is a pastor who is telling us that God was under informed. Opinion- don't believe everything you hear in church.

When attending church or reading the bible, we must understand that people with good intentions do not always get it right. Some simply have not been around long enough to gain full understanding. We must understand that pastors grow in knowledge just like everyone else. God sent Jesus to us so that we might learn about Him not so that He could learn more about us. God knows all about us. He knows more about us than we know about ourselves. The bible is based on an opinion. That opinion has become a light to the world.

The purpose of these writings is not to criticize the bible, church, or pastors. But to bring light on the increasing need to place God, His Son, and the Holy Spirit above all. Man is far from perfect. Limited in knowledge and very opinionated. With every person you see, you are looking at a different opinion.

Pray. Only God's opinion has ultimate value.

The Sinful Nature Of Man

You have heard it before. We are not sinners because we sin, we sin because we are sinner. You know many people. How many of them can you feel comfortable with giving one thousand dollars and asking them to hold it for you one week? You think you know a person, but, do you really? You expect a person to go against his/her nature. Self-interest is that which motivates most people. If you believe that most people are honest, beyond reproach, think again. Even the most honest will recline to self-interest if they can find reason to believe that they are not hurting someone else. We go through our whole lives struggling with sin. There are many who do not face this struggle. They are sinners and they could not care less. They spend their days trying to find ways to take advantage of others. To take what belongs to others. Old people, any people they can get over on. They steal, holdup, fault the government. Whatever works. These are the kind of people we have to stay away from. These are the kind of people we have to protect ourselves from. These are the kind of people we have to pray for.

But, we are not talking about those kind of people. We are talking about ourselves. People who want to do good but evil is right there with us. A slave to sin. People who do not understand what they do. What they want to do they do not do, but, what they hate they do. To the point that it is in their sinful nature. It is no longer he/she that does it, but, sin living in them. Inner struggles. We want to do right but often fail. We want to be good Christians, yet, we ask ourselves why is it that even the best Christians keep on sinning? What really happens when we become a Christian? Do we stop sinning? Does the degree of our sins lessen? It is a never ending battle. An imperfect person committing to a perfect God.

This struggle helps to better understand ourselves. It helps us to realize that we are not all we should be. That we need God's help to become the people He wants us to be. This world is full of lions and snakes ready to bring you down with every opportunity. We are not perfect. It will happen if we are not ready to defend ourselves. Pray that God will be with you through your struggle.

Image

A representation or likeness of a real or imaginary person. Your image can be protruded in a number of ways. Your personal appearance, voice, handwriting. The way you act. Have you even notice that a quiet person receives more negative judgment than a talkative person? It is important what other people think of you. It is more important what you think of yourself. Sometimes a person's image cannot be explained. He walks just like his granddaddy who he has never seen. Our Spiritual image is important.

The image of a person can be revived without ever knowing or seeing that person. No one knows what Jesus looked like. Yet, His image has been revived for thousands of years. Mary Magdalene had seen Jesus close up many times. Yet the Apostle John reports that she did not realize that it was Jesus after He had risen. She believed He was the gardener. Thomas, one of the twelve, who had also seen Jesus numerous times close up, stated "unless I see the nail marks in His hands and put my finger where the nails were, and put my hand into His side, I will not believe it." (John 20:25) Did the image of Jesus change after His Resurrection? Will our image change after we leave this world? There is an earthly body and there is a Spiritual body. We will all be changed. Just as we have borne the likeness of the earthly man, so shall we bear the likeness of the man from heaven.

Look in the mirror. That is not really you. You are seeing only the image of your earthly body. "Father, into your hands I commit My Spirit." (Luke 23:46) Your true image is within your Spirit your Soul. That which man cannot touch. Fear not one who can destroy your body. Fear He who has domination over your body and soul. The image of Jesus is greater than any who has ever walked this earth. Over two thousand years later human beings still receive inspiration from His being. Two thousand years from now they will not remember your name. But, that is secondary. Living a life pleasing in the sight of God is of primary importance. You won't do everything right, but, God knows your heart. You can feel good about yourself knowing that you are a child of God. Knowing that it is secondary what happens in this life. Because of Jesus, the best is yet to come. Your Spiritual image, your Spiritual being will soon dominate and you will live forever with your Heavenly Father.

Israel

WHY? Why did God make the decision that the Israelites would be His chosen people? They were physically weak people. Other groups could, would and did dominate them. They were spiritually weak people. Many of God's miracles would be performed before their eyes, yet, they would still not believe. They were rebellious ungratefully people. God wanted to hold Israel to high standards. They failed. The Israelites were chosen by pure grace. Grace, something received that one does not deserve. God had a decision to make. He had to find a human being to be the starting point of His purpose. He chose Abram. He put Abram to the test to be sure. He needed someone who would cleave by faith. Full of faithfulness. Who would go where he was directed and follow the commandments of God. A man who was so full of faith that God could develop his descendants to achieve His primary purpose. Through the off-springs of Abram, all men would be blessed.

Abraham's descendants were Jewish. Therefore, Israel became God's chosen people. God's ultimate plan was to bring His Son Jesus into this world. God developed the descendants of Abraham. Isaac, Jacob, David, Joseph. God had His Son come to earth because that was the only way God could get through to mankind. He tired prophets and kings. Mankind was still out of control. God had to get His message to His children. His message of everlasting love, forgiveness, Grace and Mercy. He could only do this by sending us a Redeemer, a Messiah, a Savior. Jesus was like no other person who ever lived. He was both divine and human. "The Word became flesh and made His dwelling among us." (John 1:14) Through Jesus, God spoke, communicated, directly with us. God's Son, sent to do the work of the Father. God spoke in a way we could truly understand by becoming one of us. Now, it is our ultimate purpose to become like Him.

Help!

May I help you? Everyone needs help. Some a little some a lot. But not everyone is willing to accept help. In the United States, it is lawful to physically stop a person from committing immediate suicide, but, it is not lawful to stop a person from committing slow suicide. Every 18 seconds a person in this country dies of overdose. It is not lawful to physically attack someone to keep that person from shooting up with illegal drugs. You cannot help everyone who needs help. We must be selective and aware of our limitations. When you say, may I help you, be careful. You might be taking on more than you want. The problem might be deeper than you realize. Help can be painful for both the giver and the receiver. You might be trying to put forth a sincere effort, yet, be prepared to be called some very nasty names. Do not expect immediate gratification. Abuse can be a two-way street.

Jesus came to us for the purpose of helping us. Not even Jesus could help everyone. Some would not accept His help purely because of disbelief. Some would not accept His help simply because of evilness. Regardless of the reason, Jesus was able to help only those who were willing to accept His help. Not everyone will accept the Good News, but, like Jesus we must put forth a sincere effort.

God will not force Himself on anyone. We must have the mind-set of the Good Samaritan. Some people are fooling themselves. They continue to go through the motions and give God lip service, but, they really have no desire to follow the Ways of Jesus. They have no desire to leave their comfort zone to help others. They are not fooling God. They will find this out the hard way.

We have been blessed. We have been giving Jesus to help us through the rough places in life. When we are in need of help, all we have to do is lay our all on the altar. Seek and ye shall find. Knock and the door will be open. We can only be blest and have peace and sweet rest as we yield Him our body and soul. Who can tell all the love He will send from above, and how happy our hearts will be made. Of the fellowship sweet we shall share at His feet when our all on the altar is laid.

He is here for us. He has made the opportunity available. All we have to do is go to Him and accept. The next move is yours. Ask and you shall be given. How long will the opportunity be there? Till death do we part.

What Is It All About?

What Is It All About?

Children born with serious illnesses. People being killed by acts of nature such as tornadoes and earthquakes. Innocent people murdered simply because they were in the wrong place at the wrong time. Cancer killing good people with positive promise. Death is all around us. Everywhere. Why is God permitting this to happen? Why did God give us limited time on this earth? Life is precious to us, but, is it precious to God? Life is precious to us not because our years are numbered, but, simply because of life itself. We want to hold on to something we know we will eventually lose anyway.

What is God trying to tell us by permitting this world to continue in its present condition? Does He know something that we do not know? The only pure reason for this life is to prepare to meet God. To show God that you are, at minimum, worthy of consideration. This requires a right mind set. Without the correct mind-set it is impossible to please God. What's it all about? Is it just for the moment we live? Life is short. You won't be here long and you will forget half of the years. God and His Son Jesus, you will remember till the day you die.

Jesus died for us. We should live for Him. Do you want to do something for Jesus? Live your life for Him. Step out of your comfort zone as did Jesus. Bless others as He did and your blessings will be returned ten-fold. Jesus came to us for the purpose of helping others. If we sincerely want to follow Him, if we sincerely love Him, we will use Him as our role model. We will live our lives for Jesus.

Do this in remembrance of Me.

Joy

This joy I found. The body has many elements to make it function. Some are easily visible. Others are deep within. The most important cannot be seen at all. We know they are present, but, we cannot see or touch them. Joy is one of these elements. Without it life is meaningless. Yet, this world didn't give it and this world can't take it away. Something within that holdeth the reins. Something within that banishes pain. Something within I cannot explain. All that I know there is something within. Something within that makes you feel good, comfortable, and content. Something within that makes life worth living, yet, makes death more peaceful and acceptable.

Knowing God is what it is all about. Being close to the Creator has a way of giving you peace of mind and heart. It can make you smile inside during difficult times knowing that all things work for the good in the lives of those who love God. Death is not the end. It is the beginning of an even closer relationship with our Heavenly Father. This joy I found. The world didn't give it to me and this world can't take it away. We are happy inside knowing that there is nothing that a human being can do to effect the Joy we have found in our Father, Son and the Holy Ghost.

Annotating fall on me. May the Spirit of the Holy Ghost fall on me. People are going to wonder about you. She/he always seems so content. Like he/she has something that no one can ever take way. I wonder what she/he knows that I don't know. A mind that is straight on Jesus. Knowing that the Boss Man loves you. The One who can control all. The One who can make your life something special. All you have to do is trust and have faith in Him. Without faith it is impossible to please God. Faith is not believing that God can. It is knowing that God will. He will take care of you and grant a place for you with Him in paradise.

Don't Try To Explain It

Don't Try To Explain It

It's a miracle. Never a part or result of any known natural law or agency and is therefore often attributed to a supernatural or divine source. Miraculous, wonderful and amazing, extraordinary. Apparently caused by the direct intervention of a supernatural or divine source. You cannot believe in that which is reported in the bible without believing in miracles. Jesus is a miracle. A human being who came into this world through the works of a supernatural source. Divine. Rolling back the Red Sea, restoring life to a person who was once alive, destroying a city for its many sins. This could only be done by a supernatural divine source. Trying to get an atheist to believe in the bible is like trying to get someone to believe in miracles. No one is going to become a believer by first reading the bible. You must be already visited by the Holy Spirit before you will believe in the reporting of the bible. Miracles cannot be explained. An atheist does not believe in miracles. Yet, miracles happen all around us. A two-hundred-pound man picks up the side of an automobile to free a person under it. The life of a bus driver is saved from a bullet by a bible in his shirt placed in front of his heart. A six-year old boy on his sick bed ask his father to pray with him. A five-year old boy ask a seventy-three year old man who looks ill if he is alright. A man dreams of the death of his father at the exact time it is happening. Miracles.

Why do they happen? What causes them to happen? Don't try to explain it. God is working in our lives. He is the Supernatural Divine Source. You can't touch or see Him, but you know He is there directing your life. Because of this knowledge you know that you must keep your house in order. You know that you must live a life pleasing in His sight. You know that He sees all and is a just God. He will give you exactly what you deserve. Jesus has told us this. It will not be in this life because this life is of secondary importance. The degree of glory you will receive in paradise will be determined by the way you live your life here on earth. The reason an atheist does not hear is because he does not belong to God. The kingdom of God is within you. Keep your house in order.

Appearance

It does not really matter. Or does it? Is not, what is inside that counts? How important is appearance? If a pastor walked into church on Sunday morning looking like he had been up all Saturday night, the congregation would pay more attention to his appearance than his sermon. A person's actions tell others a lot about that person. Without ever saying a word, you can relate the kind of person you appear to be just by the way you live your life. Children are watching you. They watch the way you act and the way you treat other people. The inspiration of one's presence. What others think about you is important. However, people are very self-centered. Many believe what they want to believe. The standards of people often determine the degree of respect they show others. These standards with some are very low. Believe it or not, there are some people you should not want to respect you. Nothing is more important than self-respect. There are different levels of self-respect. Some people believe that it is ok to keep something that does not belong to them as long as they can reason that they are not hurting someone else. It either belongs to you or it does not. We are very good at passing judgment on others. Beauty is only skin deep. How deep is your self-respect? Is it deeper than your skin ?

If there is one thing that Jesus could not tolerate it is a hypocrite. "Woe to you, teachers of the law and Pharisees, you hypocrites!" (Matthew 23:13) A hypocrite is a person who is not the same in-side as on the outside. "You clean the outside of the cup and dish, but inside they are full of greed and self-indulgence." (Matthew 23:25) You go to church, sing pretty songs of praise, but, you never think about doing anything for anyone other than yourself. Do you think Jesus would consider you a hypocrite?

What should a leader look like? Why would people not accept Jesus as a spiritual leader? They wanted someone who appeared to be strong and powerful. Someone who would over-power the Romans, the people who were enslaving them, and set them free. They wanted a Jewish King. Jesus was not the type of savior they were looking for. They wanted a savior not a Savior. He was a Savior who used His power compassionately for the sake of others. A Savior who used His powers to feed the hungry and heal the sick. He was not concerned about a powerful image a powerful appearance.

The one primary lesson we must learn from Jesus is that He placed the Will of God before all considerations. Even His Will was secondary to the Will of His Father. I want, is a statement we make from birth. Our most important want is to want to be more like Jesus. No one said the road would be easy. We should live each day thinking about one question. How do I appear to Jesus?

Government

In a democracy, government is by the people and for the people. Decisions are made by the people by electing leaders who decide what is best for all. If the majority of the people do not agree with the leader, they replace the leader. Majority rules. Government tells us what we can to and what we cannot do. Government sets the rules and the penalties for not following those rules. Sometimes government is wrong. Slavery is an example. One wrong decision can hurt millions of people.

As a Christian, we have a double edge sword to deal with. We have to live with other people so we have to obey the laws of society. However, there is a source more powerful than human government. A source that is never wrong. That tells us what we are permitted to do and not permitted to do. A source that is for the people, but, not by the people. A source that has already made all decisions. That we cannot change when we disagree. The majority does not rule. A source that also tells us the penalty for not following the rules.

Government is important. You cannot have the blessings of God without the government of God. A decision that benefits the majority of the people is not necessary correct. The right decision can only be made when the Will of God is followed. As a Christian, there will be numerous occasions when you have to make the decision do I follow God's laws or those of man. Not following the laws of man can cause serious hardship. But you have been told to not fear he who can destroy your body. Fear He who can destroy your body and your Soul.

There is something more important than this life. He who has not found something worth dying for does not deserve to live. That something more important than this life is God. He who gave life and He who has the authority and power to take it back. There is no government with more authority than the government of God. Do not conform to this world. The Will of Almighty God will have the last word. Government for His people.

Coaching

There are many members of a person. Mind, Body and Spirit. All must work together to achieve a common goal. That life goal must be carefully defined. This is the first challenge. If this decision is not all it should be, nothing else will be correct. The majority of people pick something material as their life goal. If you live in New York, you will find it very difficult going to San Francisco heading East. How many people do you know who state a goal in life?

Most Americans are over-weight. Because it takes effort and sacrifice to control your body. In life, we cannot be concerned with what taste good. It also takes effort and sacrifice to control your mind. When your mind determines your direction in life, your goals, you are in trouble. Your heart is the most important member. When it stops, you die. When it stops telling you that which is good, you die. If it is leading you in the wrong direction, you will not win this race. You will be running away from the finish line.

Remember the four H's. Heart, Head, Hands, Habit. All must start with the heart. This is what I want to do, the kind of person I want to be. Then it goes to the head. This is how I am going to do it. Then the hands. Getting it done. When doing good becomes a habit in life, you have arrived. You have won this race.

It takes a lot of wisdom. God sent Jesus to be your coach. When determining your goal in life, think of Him first. He will help you determine your life goal. He will help you plan, organize, direct, control, and co-ordinate your life to end up at your desired destination. WISDOM.

Jesus lead me. Guide me all the way. Lord if you lead me, I cannot stray. Lord let me walk each day with thee. My Father, please lead me.

Keeping It Fresh

Keeping It Fresh

It will spoil if you do not give it attention. You put food in your refrigerator to keep it fresh. You water vegetables and flowers to keep them fresh. Everything of value must receive attention. Everything of value must be put to its purpose, used, to remain functional. Do not start up an automobile for a few years and it will give you problems. Use it or lose it. Keeping food cold will work for a limited time. Everything of value must be permitted to serve its purpose.

Your Religion is the same. Why was the church, temple, important to God and Jesus? We have heard a thousand sermons and read thousands of words. There is very little that a preacher can say that we have not heard or read before. So why go to church? We go to church to keep our Religion fresh. Everyone, including God, likes to be praised. God loves it. We go to church to jointly praise the Lord. To let Him know that we appreciate His constant care for us. That is the reason we read the same words in the bible over and over. To help us keep our minds straight on Jesus. If we do not, this world will turn us into something less than we should be. It is easier to adopt that which is bad than good. Stay around a bad person long enough and your behavior will suffer. We must keep Jesus fresh in our minds. Thank Him when we get up for permitting us another day and when we go to bed for helping us through another day.

We must use that which He has taught us. Using it is a key way to keep our Religion fresh. Again, everything of value must be permitted to serve its purpose. Is your Religion valuable to you? Use it or lose it. Follow JESUS.

I'm Good

How are you? I'm good. How many times have you heard that reply? The question is, are you good by God's standards? An atheist is not good. A person who serves a god or gods other than the true God is not good. A person who serves material things such as house, car, or money more than God is not good. A person who claims to be a Christian, love God, but, lives his/her life like an atheist is not good. Even a person who would not hurt a fly. Loves family and takes care of all responsibilities. Helps other at every opportunity, but, does not have God in his/her live is not good.

We serve a jealous and demanding God. You cannot ignore God and be considered good. God don't play that. Indifference toward God, like following false gods, is an evil that is worthy of God's judgment. All of the above are act of disobedience and all will be subject to consequences. It is not a matter of sin. You are going to do that rather you want to or not. Sin is a part of your nature. King David, with all of his many sins, was considered after God's own heart because he sincerely went to God seeking forgiveness. Repentance. Jesus told Peter, unless he repents, he to shall parish. It is not the sins we commit that lead us to disaster and destruction. It is the failure to repent and turn to our forgiving God.

God's standards, not our own, are to be accepted and sought. Think about the wars that people have started and all the human beings who have suffered because of them. The righteous often suffer because of the wicked. Leave it to God. Trust and believe in Him and He will provide a hiding place for your Soul. A life of faith that seeks God and His righteousness will be rewarded hopefully in this life and with assurance in eternal. There is only one future. With our Lord forever.

Importance

You are no more important to others than they are to you. Some pastors need to learn that. You are no more important to God than God is to you. This is a very difficult statement to accept. You can try to do the right things in life, but, if God is not in your life you have sinned. You cannot ignore God and expect to receive His Joy. God don't play that. We serve a jealous demanding God. He demands obedience, respect and attention. You cannot receive His blessings without accepting His government. Read the Ten Commandments. For almost one half of the ten commandments, God is talking about Himself. You shall have no other gods before Me. You shall not make for yourself an idol. You shall not misuse the name of the Lord. Observe the Sabbath day.

It was not meant to be easy. It takes work and disciple to stay in God's good graces. If you do not keep your mind straight on Jesus, you will slip. Getting into heaven is not easy. Everything good takes hard work. The better it is the more work that is required. Can you think of anything better than heaven? It takes more than just going to church and getting emotional. Following Jesus is not an easy path. Much is required of you.

Most people will not go to heaven. Some Christians will not go to heaven. God has set difficult requirements to enter His Kingdom. Most of us will not make it. Most of us have more value for what's happening now than for eternity. That is what this life is. A test. A "C" average might get you through the gates, but, do not think that you will receive the same Joy as others who have scored higher. The test is difficult, but, don't let it be because of a lack of effort on your part. The final decision is His, but, put your two cents on the table. You might far short, but, it will not be because of a lack of effort. We serve a just God. Keep your mind straight on JESUS.

Tightrope

It only takes one lie to make you a liar. There is no such thing as a little sin. A terrorist kills numerous people. An atheist states that there is no God. It is not the sin. It is the defiance of God. You are walking a tightrope from birth. You were born a sinner. You are not a sinner because you sin, you sin because you are a sinner. I am glad I'm not like him. How can anyone do something like that? By making statements like these, you are revealing that you are satisfied with your present level of sin. It is not for us to determine the degree of sin. That is God's territory. We will all die because we are all sinners. Sin is the cause of death. Sin occurs when we disobey the Will of God.

Sin is a part of your nature. You will walk a tightrope in your fight against sin all of your life. You will not win all of the battles, but, you can win the war. All you have is who you are. What you do or accomplish in life is not as important as who you are. The kind of person you are. That will be of primary importance in God's judgment. You cannot be all that you should be without giving God the Glory. There are some good people in this world who will not go to heaven because they did not give God the Glory. You cannot ignore God and receive His joy. It is never too late to change. Every Saint has a past and every sinner has a future. You are going to sin rather you want to or not. The magic word is REPENTANCE. Once you learn the value of this word, you no longer have to walk the tightrope of life. Just do your best to do God's Will. To live a life pleasing in His sight. When you find that you have not won a battle, go to him and ask for help. He loves you. All of His decisions will be with your best interest at heart. Trust in Him. It is not believing that He can it is knowing that God will take care of you.

Make-Up Your Bed

Make-Up Your Bed

Oh, what a dream I had last night. Dreams. Some are good and some are bad. We have no control over them. Are they telling us something? Is there something in our sub-conscious that we do not want to face when we are awake? Is the Holy Spirit speaking to us at a time when we are most accessible? Mystery. Some dreams we cannot remember when we wakeup. Some we can. Some dreams are not as obvious as they might seem. We have to ask ourselves how they apply to our lives. In many ways dreams are like life when we are awake. There are some things in life that are a mystery which we are not suppose to have the answers. In which we are not suppose to understand. Over which we have no control. We must only accept them and ask ourselves how they apply to our lives.

Jesus told us to get ready and stay ready. He told us that the end will come like a thief in the night. Was He talking about death? A terrorist kills forty-nine people. Did all of them deserve to die at such an early age? Mystery. Like a thief in the night. We say that they had no warning, but, did they? Jesus warned them, as he warned us all. We must get ready and stay ready to leave this life without notice. Tomorrow was meant for some, but, tomorrow may never come.

Death is a part of life. Our tomorrows have already been planned for us if we act right. God wants you with Him. However, He is going to accept you only under certain conditions. Only if you believe and live your life like you believe. Make-up your bed. Each morning, thank Him for permitting you to see another day. Ask for His help to live that day as He wants you to live. Tomorrow might be the day He calls your name. Get ready and stay ready.

Father

He who contributes to bringing a person into this world. The reason we do anything is as important as what we do. An earthly father might contribute out of love. Some contribute only out of personal satisfaction. A lack of responsibility has become a major problem. Women are at fault as much as men. How can you contribute to bringing someone into this world for which you will have no responsibility? It is good for us to protect ourselves from such acts and such people. There are two definitions of the word father. One with and one without responsibility. One with and one without love. Only with love can a father become a dad. There can be no love without responsibility. Yet, without love, you are a walking dead man.

True love. Total responsibility. We call Him our Heavenly Father. He has permitted us life for a purpose. We all have the same purpose. To praise His Holy Name. To help His people. A dad is someone who is always there to help you. Who has a strong desire to protect you from all harm. Who you can turn to in times of need and in times of joy. There are no limits to his efforts to provide that which is good. You would put your life in his hands out of trust, respect, and love. A father talks to his child. He must receive the co-operation of the child. If he does not, he will punish the child. He does not force the child to do anything because in the long run it will do no good.

There is only one God. The Creator of Heaven and Earth. The Creator of you. Your Father your Dad. The One who brought you into this world and the One who will take you out. He has the right to do so. You belong to Him. You have been bought with a price. Your life belongs to Him. He gave you life and He told you how to live your life. He who has ears, let him hear. He is not going to force you to do anything. He will accept only those who love and obey Him.

The decision is yours. You are going somewhere after you leave here. You decide where. Accepting and obeying Him will also make this life more peaceful and content. It's a win win situation. You can't go wrong with Jesus. Praise His Holy Name.

Stormy Weather

Stormy Weather

Don't know why there is no sun up in the sky. Stormy weather. Why is it that bad things happen to good people? That's life, flying high in April, shot down in May. It does not matter how good you are when it comes to trouble. You will have your share of it regardless. How you are mentally prepared to deal with it is what matters. It's all in the mind.

To us, death is trouble. We know it is going to happen, yet, we are never prepared. The deceased has gone back to the Creator. We can't cry about that. We cry for ourselves. We have lost a loving relationship. That is what life is all about. Relationships. Your relationship with Jesus. No person can live in this world alone. We love and we hate. There are somethings in life that we are not meant to understand. Some people are born with a silver spoon in their mouths. Others are born into poverty. A son kills his parents because they would not let him have a party in their home. Then he has the party with their bodies locked in another room. The silver spoon did him no good because God was not in his life.

We are given opportunity and resources. It is up to us to take advantage of them. God is a resource. This resource can help us in many ways. To handle our highs and lows. To understand that in life what goes up must come down. What is born must die. This resource helps us code with life. Believing that there is One who loves us and who is in total control.

Why is it that bad things happen to good people? Why is there so much suffering in this world? There is One who has all the answers. We can only trust in His judgment. In His love. All things work for the good of those who know, love and trust Him. You make the choice. God does not send anyone to Hades.. People decide they want to go to hades by the way they live their lives. Without God's leadership we will all go to Hades.

Know your place in life. Know your limitations. Know who is in control of your life. Know that He loves you. Nothing else matters.

Think

Just follow God. Just believe and trust Him like children trust their parents. God is the author of the bible. This means that He has edited every word. There are those who deeply believe this to be true. No one can prove them wrong. They believe one should believe in God and follow the commandments of God blindly. It's a no brainer. Don't think.

God gave you a brain to use without restrictions. Think about it. Will God's way make your life better? Will God's way give you more peace and contentment? First, you have to decide what kind of person you want to be. This is the most important decision you will ever make. Will His way help make you that kind of person? God has given us valuable tools to use to make our lives better. Those tools are in the raw form. We have to plant the seed and harvest so that His gift will have purpose. It takes a strong mind to employ these gifts to achieve wisdom. 75% of children who grow up and leave home do not keep God in their lives. Maybe some parents did not think to employ God's gifts in a meaningful way. The employment of God's gifts can have important meaning to our lives and to the lives of others.

God gave you a mind a brain to use in all situations. Use what God has given you. Think! Why does God care so much about me? Think! Why does God love me when I have never done anything for Him? Think! What kind of person do I want to be? Think! Will my life be better with or without Him as a part of it? God wants you to think about your alternatives. God is waiting for your decision. He is not going to wait forever.

A mind is a terrible thing to waste. THINK.

The Greater Sin

A terrorist kills 49 people who he does not even know. An atheist says there is no God. Both have committed the sin of showing defiance toward God. Which of the two has committed the greater sin? Many, at first, would say that they have committed sins that are equal. But have they? A person who believes in white supremacy says he hates black people. Another person who believes in white supremacy says he hates blacks then kills ten black people. Hate is in the hearts of both. Are their sins equal?

Scripture has informed us that talk alone will not satisfy God. We have to walk our talk. We have to live the life we sing about in our songs. Jesus told us that He will reward us according to that which we deserve. According to our degree of goodness. All is not equal in heaven. The degree of Joy you receive will be determined by what you do or don't do in this life. By what you deserve. This tells us that God does measure what we do. God does determine our degree of sin. Some believe sin is sin. Others believe some sins are a greater defiance of God.

It is not for us to step into God's territory. It is not for us to determine the degree of sin. It is only for us to do our best to avoid sin at every level. Society determines the degree by which people disobey the law. Christians live life under the Laws of God. We have but one life to live. To God be the GLORY.

Decisions

The most important decision that we will ever make is the kind of person we want to be. Good, bad, or ugly. Becoming an ugly person is not as negative as becoming a bad person, but, it is headed in the same direction. All future decisions must take into account your most important decision. Many decisions are made with good intentions. A decision that is best for the majority of the people must be a good decision. Or, is it. The problem is that it might have been made with human values as priority. No decision can be correct without the consideration of God's values. It takes wisdom to make important correct decisions. The kind of person you want to be is an important decision. That decision will direct the path of your life. Wisdom is the art of thinking like God, not like man. Jesus told Peter, get behind me Satan, because Peter was thinking like man not like God. One cannot correctly make the most important decision in life without wisdom. One cannot display wisdom by looking at life through the eyes of man. There is a very simply reason for this. Life will end. One can only display wisdom by looking at life through the eyes of God because only He controls eternity.

Jesus came to us because He had the desire to help people. He knew that the most important way to help was to let people know about the goodness of God. To let us know about eternity because all else will end. Jesus give us the Great Commission because it is important to share our knowledge. You can't take it with you when you go. What is not given is lost.

It is amazing the number of people that go to church on Sunday morning, yet, the name of Jesus never comes out of their mouths until they return to church the next Sunday. Jesus is their secret. When they die, they will take that secret to the grave with them. If it were not important, do you think Jesus would have wasted His last breath on this earth to instruct us of our duty. There is no question mark after the last sentence because there is no question to our responsibility if we are Christians. If you call yourself a Christian, then act like one. Fulfill your responsibility. If you are ashamed of the name of Jesus, stop playing games. He will not play games with your name come judgment day.

What kind of person do you want to be? In the name of Jesus. AMEN.

Scrutiny

Who is the boss? The one thing that most of us do not like is to be told what to do. Yet, we are subject to the instructions of others from childhood. Mom, dad, school teacher, team coach. Even when you drive your car, you must follow instructions. Stop, go, speed limits. The government states what you should and should not do and what will happen to you if you disobey.

Is there really any difference in the way the government handles things and the way God handles things? Both give you commands. Both tell you how to live your life and what the consequences will be if you do not obey. The government does not always see you when you disobey. But, God sees everything you do. We are always under His scrutiny. Be careful, I'm watching you. Your life is not your own. You have been bought with a price. God has given you life and told you how to live it. He has also told you want will happen if you do not obey. God controls you. He dominates your life. You live every moment of your life under the scrutiny of God. That's a good thing. It can become an enjoyable challenge just to know that He who is grading the test has the character of forgiveness.

God knows what is in your heart. He knows your areas of weakness. He loves you. He wants you to succeed. He has a place for you with Him in eternity. I would rather live in God's world than live without Him in mine.

Human Race

Human Race

Discrimination has been a major problem in this society for more than two thousand years. Racial discrimination. I don't consider you an equal because you don't look like me. Gender discrimination. I will not pay you the same wage as he because you are a female. Religious discrimination. I will not associate with you because you do not believe as I believe. Jesus came to this earth to let us know that God loves all of us equally. There need not be a race for the love, grace and mercy of God. When Jesus walked this earth, he had many human problems to address. Jews were very discriminatory people. God punished them many times for their sins. God permitted other Nations to enslave Israel to teach them that disrespect for God would be taken seriously. Jews did not like Sarmatia people because they were considered half-breeds. They would not associate with them. They would not eat or drink with them. When Jews were enslaved, they had sexual relations with non-Jews. Babies who were not pure Jewish were born. If you were not a pure Jewish, you were not acceptable.

Discrimination has been a part of religious life for a long time. White people would attend church on Sunday morning. Then, they would take their lawn chairs to the park to watch as naked blacks were hung from trees and their bodies burned. Religion folks. The teachings of Jesus had no meaning to these people. The law stood by watching. Society is close to change. They don't hang black people any more. They just shoot unarmed black men down in the streets.

We must understand that the life of Jesus means nothing to some people. Discrimination is not always a bad thing. Separation is not always a bad thing. There are some people it would be best to stay away from. There is a fine line here. This line has many questions attached that can only be answered by answering one question. What would Jesus have me do? Following Jesus can be difficult and complicated. That is where prayer comes in. That is where the Holy Spirit comes in.

A wise man once said, if we do not learn to live together as brothers, we will parish together as fools. The bond is Jesus Christ. Only our Lord has the answer to this problem of the human race.

Gifts From The Lord

Gifts From The Lord

God has given each of us a special gift. It was not His intention for us to be a trick of all trades and a master of none. It is for us to be very good at a few things. It is amazing when we think of a blind person or a seven- year- old mastering the piano. A person with a photographical memory. A person with a special gift with numbers or spelling. Some can run at great speeds. Others can jump great heights.

We must recognize and accept our special gifts. Some gifts are not as obvious as others. An excellent public speaker. A person who has a way with people. Who has an unique way of helping others. All are God given gifts unique to each individual. We should thank God for the great things He has done. We should also recognize and show respect for His love and power. There are so many things that were not made and cannot be controlled by man. These things are only under the control of God. Human beings should be careful not to step into God's territory.

The gender of a person is the decision of our Heavenly Father. Humans show a disrespect to our God when they try to change His decisions. You were not meant to be what you want to be. You were meant to be what God wants you to be. Father know best. He has made you a certain way for a purpose. Accept it. Show Him the respect He is due. Develop your gift. Grow in His Spirit. He gave birds wings to fly. He gave life, a special gift and a brain to you to fly higher. When you fly, never forget the Giver. The greatest challenge we have is to develop our special gifts WITHIN the territory granted to us by God Almighty.

God's Sovereignty

It is difficult to accept anything without understanding. As humans, reason, understanding, logic are the bases of our direction. We have heard the old saying if it sounds too good to be true it probably isn't. We see terrible things going on in this world. Most caused by other humans. But sometimes things happen and we will never find out why. Babies are born with less than normal physical conditions. Rain and wind kill people. Someone dies from lightning every week. There is no understanding as to why bad things happen to good people or why those who have done nothing to deserve it have to suffer.

As Christians, we understand that we have limited knowledge for one very simply reason. That reason being God's Sovereignty. We can only accept these truths. The incomprehensibility of God. We will never fully understand God. He has told us that our ways are not His ways. The apostle Paul told Israel that being a descended of Abraham did not make them truly Israel in a spiritual sense. It is not a matter of birth. It is a matter of faith in the Messiah. We Christians must understand that going to church each Sunday and singing pretty songs of praise does not mean that we will be saved. You might think you are saved, but, only God knows. Many people you see in church on Sunday morning will never make it to heaven. God has made His sovereign choice before you are born. He knows in advance everything you will go through in life. He knows what problems you will have and what your decisions will be. God has made the decision as to your acceptance into heaven before you were born into this world. He has chosen whom He will bless. This might be hard to take and even harder to understand. God has mercy on whom He chooses and hardens those He chooses to harden. Yes, it is beyond our full comprehension, but, He uses it to accomplish His perfect will. We rest in His grace. We are dependent on God's mercy. He has, in His infinite wisdom, chosen to be merciful on a world of sinners. His mercy has nothing to do with human merit. For that reason, when you get to heaven the only person you should be surprised to see is yourself.

God does not need or want your understanding. He is God all by Himself. He does whatever He wants to do. He is at work in our lives to bring eternal glory to Himself. God is God. We cannot judge Him. He acts sovereignly to carry out His Holy purpose. We can only be glad that we serve a just and loving God.

Live The Life

We tell the world that we love our Heavenly Father. We attend prayer and praise services, bible study, Sunday school, church services. We sing pretty songs of praise. Animism. The belief in the existence of spirit and soul, as distinct from matter. Then we return to our lives of anxiety. Disturbance of mind regarding some uncertain event, misgiving, worry. Fear and apprehension regarding the future. The way we live our lives is evidence of our faith. That building we go to on Sunday morning is not the church. The people in it are the church. The church does not exist only for its members. The purpose of the church is to serve the community through the power of the Holy Spirit. The people of the church must serve the community. They, however, cannot service others until they understand their own purpose for living. They cannot serve others until they accept the Lord into their lives seven days a week not just on Sunday. When they are in their houses not just the House of God. God must control our minds each day of our lives. Only through the Spirit of God can we over power the anxiety of life. Once we accept His promise to love, protect, and provide a place for us with Him in eternity, we will live our lives with peace and without anxiety. We will Live the Life we sing about in our songs.

Death

Death

Death is the end for some people. Death is the beginning for others. Death strikes 1.25 million people on this earth every day. To non-believers, it's poison is deadly. Non-believers are the walking dead. They are not lifeless, but they are not responsive to their Maker. They are without spiritual life. It is also true that some Christians are so eternally minded that they are of little use to God's world. God sent Jesus to us for two primary purposes. God wants us to accept and love Him. God wants us to live our lives more abundantly. We can only please God by doing both. Only by doing both will He open the doors of Paradise to each of us.

The Holy Ghost comes into the lives of people only when those people are ready to receive. Some-times it is instant. Other times, over a period of time, the Holy Spirit will keep reappearing until you start to live your life for God mentally and physically. The Spirit has an effect on your heart, mind, and hands. Living your life for God is much more than yourself. Jesus was much more than Himself. His desire was to bring others to God. Some of us are so focused on ourselves with respect to God that we don't think about anyone else. If we truly want to be more and more like Jesus every day, we will accept the belief that living for God means serving Him both internally and externally.

Quoting scripture will not bring others to God. Telling others how God has changed your life will. Reading the bible will not make a person a Christian. You are the bible. You are the church. Do you want to get to heaven? You can't get there by keeping Jesus to yourself. Jesus came here to bring people to God. There was nothing more important to Him. What does that tell you?

Why?

Why is it that good people have such hard times? Why is it that human beings suffer? Why does God permit Satan to continue to control the lives of so many? God has the power to destroy the devil with one word. God has the power to end all forms of evil temptation. Why does He not exercise His power? Maybe God wants you to suffer. Maybe God wants you to go through some hard times. Think about it and be honest with yourself. If you did not have trouble, how would it affect your relationship with God? If you knew that there was no death, that you would live forever, would God still be the center of your life? You want to say yes, but, the fact is that most human beings would not give God the attention they should if they did not have to. Yes, you fear the power of the judgement of God. You might want to call this fear by another name like respect, but, you fear God's judgement.

Heaven is a beautiful place so I have been told. I once met a man who said that he had been to heaven for a short period of time. He said, in heaven there is no pain, suffering and no tears. There are people, here on earth, who want to make this life like heaven. Stop! It is not and it will never be that way. We read in Scripture that we die because of sin. We are all sinners, therefore, we must all die. Adam and Eve had something to do with that. It is true that suffering brings us closer to God. It is true that hard times bring us closer to God. We would like to think that God would have the same place in our lives even if all were perfect and there was no death, but, the effort would be much more difficult. It is very difficult for a human being to stop thinking about his or her self. The Greatest Commandment is to love God with all your heart, mind, soul, and strength. How many of us really do this? How many of us still have in the back of our minds, what's in it for me?

You think you are a Christian. You think you are saved. The truth is that you have a lot of work to do. You are not all you should be. Prayer can help you. Prayer can help set your mind and heart right. God can help you to become all that you should be. Trying to overcome the negatives of being a human being requires more than yourself. That's the reason Jesus told us to pray and keep on praying because we all need a lot of help.

God Don't Play That

God Don't Play That

There are approximately 7 billion people living in this world. 38% of them are Christians. Christianity is the largest faith in the world. 90% of Christians live in only ten countries. The other 10% live in countries most of whom do not permit Christians to worship openly. Many of these people fear for their lives. More Christians live in the U.S.A than in any other one country. There are around 155 countries. Only about ten can be considered Christian. 145 out of 155 countries do not believe in God or do not believe that Jesus is the Son of God. That tells me one thing. A lot of people are not going to heaven. 60% of those living on the face of this earth today are not going to heaven. Many people who consider themselves Christians, who consider themselves saved, will not make it to heaven. Some people you see in church almost every Sunday morning singing pretty songs of praise, amen, showing a lot of emotion will be on the outside looking in. They hear the name of Jesus numerous times on Sunday. The next Sunday they hear the name of Jesus numerous times. What about the days in-between each Sunday? How many times do they hear or speak the name of Jesus during those six days? Somewhere between zero and none. They go to church and act like Jesus is all the world to them. Then they leave church go home and turn on the television. Jesus came to earth for one primary reason. To help people. Nothing was more important to Him. Before leaving, He give us the Great Commission. Go out and tell every Nation the GOOD NEWS. Baptizing them in the name of the Father, the Son, and the Holy Ghost. The primary problem with most Christians is they will not talk about Jesus outside of the walls of the church. Why? I don't know. I don't know if they even know. But they better find out real soon because tomorrow was meant for some, but, tomorrow may never come and there is plenty of room down below.

The Game

The Game

Numerous people like competitive sports. Most sports require physical activity. Most sports are easy to understand. You know the rules of the game. You know the amount of time you will have to accomplish your goal. You know your opponent. You have had an opportunity to scout your opponent. You know the strengths and weaknesses of your opponent. In life we also have an opponent. The problem is that Satan does not play by the rules. He will come at you any way he can. It is his goal to attack your heart, mind and body. He will try to find out your breaking point. Compromise your values and your character. How much will it take to put her/him under? Once he gets a piece of your character, he is like termites. He will keep eating away until the house falls down.

Life in many ways is different from sports. There are no rules. We can't scout our opponent. We do not really know his weaknesses. The primary problem is that we do not know when the game will end. If we are behind when the final buzzer sounds, we will be in trouble. We know we are sinners and that we will not do everything right. We know that fouls will be called. But, we do not always know the score. God wants it that way. He is telling us to get ahead and stay ahead in this game of life or suffer the consequents. We might not know the score, but, we have a good ideal as to rather we are ahead or behind. Some of us might have to go into a full court press to get back in the game.

One of the biggest problems we have is thinking we are more than we are. Oh, I can take a licking and keep on ticking. Not smart. If you are an alcoholic, stay away from the bars. If you are a homosexual, stay away from him or her. Why do more people get shot in bars than in church? If your butt was home in bed at 2 a.m. instead of at that night club shaken it, it might still be in one piece. God gave you a brain, if you do not use it look in the mirror and you will see the reason why.

We don't know why bad things happen to good people, but, good people have to stop helping them happen. If he wants to drive his car and life like a fool, just get out of his way. Staying away from trouble is a difficult job, but, God gave you the equipment to handle the job successfully.

Reason To Believe

Reason To Believe

Some believe that there is no place for reason or logic in religion. We walk by faith not by sight. Many believe that Scripture should be taken at face value. Maybe they are right. Have you ever heard a law enforcement officer use the phrase (reason to believe)? He is saying, based on the evidence to date the following conclusions have been made. It takes reason and logic to evaluate evidence.

Religion is not based on blind faith. It is reasonable to believe there is a God. Look at all of the elements that man did not create and over which he has no control. This fact makes it reasonable to believe that the power of the Creator has no limits. His powers go deeper than the eye can see. We read certain events in Scripture that seem impossible. They are impossible for man not for God. I AM THAT I AM. (THAT I AM) means nothing contributed to His existence. He is the beginning and the end. This might be difficult for some humans to accept and understand, but, it is the bases of the Christian faith.

We are under the control of someone or something we will never fully understand. Yet, we have reason to believe that whatever this power is, He is the Creator of heaven and earth.

To God Be The GLORY.

Temptation

Temptation can be good or bad. Too often we speak of the word as if it only represents evil. Temptation gives us an open view as to the condition of our hearts. As humans, we are weak. We must work hard to do the right thing. Doing the bad thing or doing nothing is easy. We are tempted to take the easy way out. Staying on the battlefield for our Lord takes effort. Once we enlist, we have made a commitment to serve until death do us part. God has told us our responsibilities as His warriors. We are fighting a war each and every day of our lives. The enemy is known by a number of names. More names than anyone in the bible other than Jesus. Devil, Satan, Lucifer, Abaddon, Accuser, Adversary, Beast, Dragon. The list goes on and on, but, his mission is very specific. He wants your soul.

Just as the word temptation is too often used to represent evil, the word angel is too often used to represent good. There are good and bad angels. Lucifer was once an angel. He was an archangel. A leader of other angels. He started to smell himself and believed that he could overthrow Almighty God. God kicked him out of heaven and he landed on earth. A fallen angel. An angel of the bottomless pit. Good angels are our invisible helpers and comforters. They helped Jesus when He was tempted by Satan for forty days. They will help us if we believe and trust in them. That is the major problem. There are many who do not believe. Many who are too weak to fight off the temptations of the devil. Or, they are too stupid to realize that they are even in a war. Lucifer and his demons, other fallen angels, are at work every day in their attempt to take-a-way your Salvation. They know they can never win the war. Jesus has already given us the Victory. But, they don't care. They are evil. They will steal every soul that they can. They will steal your soul if you do not use Jesus to defend you. When they see that you are protected by Jesus, they will go away and find some unprotected soul to attack.

Jesus died for our sins. What this means is that He has given us a means of defense. He knows our adversary will never give up. He knew this evil was casted to the earth from heaven and will continue the fight until eternity. We have a way out. This beast will not be destroyed during our life time, but, we can hold him at bay. He is helpless against the armor of Jesus. Show him the Cross and he will run. To hades where he belongs. He does not belong in your heart and mind. Jesus will help you in your fight against evil.

Master

We really don't like anyone telling us want to do. When we think of the word master, we think of a person who has the power to force his will upon us. To make us do whatever he wants. The word master, like many other words, has more than one meaning. A master chef is one who has great skills in his/her profession. Like the word fear, the word master does no always have to be negative.

It is all the way we look at things. Even people. You can let another person get on your last nerve or you can exercise patience and maybe help. That's life. When we keep in the back of our minds the love that God has for us and the home He has prepared for us, we are able to handle stressful moments in our lives with a smile.

We know that our lives are only temporary. It's all in what you believe. Why did God permit this to happen to me? Is this an example of His love? There is something you need to know. You don't care more about your life than does God. There is a difference. God wants you to grow in His Spirit. One way you can do this is by going to Him in stressful situations. He wants you to depend on Him. You can handle any situation any grief when you permit God to be the Master of your life. The key word is permit. There is no force.

Another word that can have other than a negative meaning is the word slavery. Scripture tells us that we will be a slave to something in our lives. Good or evil. God or Satan. You decide. There is no middle ground. By selecting one, you eliminate the other. You can't be a good person without God in your life. You might try to do all the right and good things, but, you have left out the most important right, GOD.

He has all power in His hands. He loves you. Live your life each day with God in the back of your mind. At the top of each hour say to yourself, God is in the back of my mind. You will see the light of the world open before your eyes. You will live each day with peace and contentment. God is in control of your life. It's a wonderful world, it's a wonderful life when you believe God is in control. Let God lead you.

My Cup Runneth Over

Why do you go to church so often? Why do you read the same words in the bible over and over again? You have heard a thousand sermons and read thousands of words. Do you really think that you are going to hear something in church that you have not heard or read before?

The human mind is complicated. It is capable of doing the extraordinary, It also has limitations. Often that which is important must be repeated numerous times before it is accepted. You hear it. You read it. You think you have it. But, not really. Your actions state otherwise. Putting that which we think we believe into action is very difficult for human beings. Remember the four H's. Heart, Head, Hands, Habit. Only when following God's way becomes a habit can we truly say I got it.

Fill a glass full of chocolate milk. Slowly pour a pitcher of clear water into the glass. Soon the glass of chocolate milk turns into clear water. This is the way the Holy Spirit works. You can't rush it. It takes time for the human heart and mind to truly accept God's way. It grows on you. We go to church and read His word in order to slowly receive the Holy Spirit into our lives. Along the way, we become more and more able to live the life we sing about in our songs.

God's Spirit is working on and in you. You are growing in His Spirit every day. Keep growing and you will become the person God wants you to be. The cherished child of the Creator of Heaven and Earth.

Make Up Your Bed II

Make Up Your Bed II

We learn a lot from our parents. Not only what they say, but, also how they live their lives. Not only the big, but, also the small things that they do. The saying, do as I say not as I do, is not a very good slogan for parents. How can you expect a child not to smoke when she/he is watching you do it every day?

The actions of a parent will make an impression on a child even without that child knowing it. You are being watched. The way you treat others. The words you use. Even things that are small can make a good or bad impression on a child. How you keep house. When your mother practices that there is a place for everything and everything should be in its place, the child learns without a word being spoken.

Making up your bed in the morning is more than the physical act. It includes the recognition of God's Grace in your life. He didn't have to do it. He didn't have to carry you through another day and permit you one more day of life. We too often take the Grace of God for granted as if we are entitled. God does not owe you anything. What do you owe God? You cannot owe someone something that you can never pay back.

Each and every morning give God the Glory for the things He has done in your life. Thank God for His Grace and Mercy. Thank you Jesus, for You brought me from a mighty long way.

What's It All About II

Kindergarten, grade school, high school, college and beyond. Bible study and church. Why do we go through all of this? There is a very simple answer. The quality of life. The physical quality of life is very important to us all. There are two parts to the quality of life. To some the physical part dominates. Big house, luxury car, steak, authority. To some these are of major importance.

Why do we see poor children in third world countries smiling and laughing? Could it be that they don't know anything other than what they see. This is the way it is suppose to be. This tells us that there is more to the quality of life than just the physical. Your mind, not your body, determine your quality of life. This is a fact regardless of the amount of money you have. It's all in the mind.

One of the most important factors that faith in God gives us is mental comfort. We understand that this to must pass. We understand that God is in control and that nothing can be out of control when God is in control. We KNOW that He loves us. We have no anxiety. No worry about our future or the future of a love one because we believe our future is in the palm of the hand of Almighty God. We don't have to have complete understanding. We have FAITH in He who cares for us beyond all reason. He is the reason we can handle anything that happens to us in this life. When God is for us, it matters not who is against us. Even Lucifer. It's all in the mind. Smile, God is in control of your life.

Youth

Don't you wish you had some? How many times have you said, I wish I knew thirty years ago what I know now? It's too bad youth has to be wasted on the young. Walk into church on Sunday morning and you can count the people between 20 and 39 years of age on your fingers. This age group are still receiving the blessings of God, but, to them life is more important. Everything to them is a new experience. Heaven can wait. Then they start to develop. They receive some hard knocks in life. There is an old saying, man learn from experience, but, a wise man learns from the experiences of other. There are fewer hard knocks that way.

Hard knocks bring us closer to God. It's a good life to be free and explore the unknown. Till the hard times and we learn we must face them alone. But remember God still loves you and if you wonder why. Well just wake-up and kiss the good life good-bye. God is always there for us. Even when we are too mentally limited to recognize His presence. He knows our needs. If we could only, through each stage of life, recognize our need for Him.

Early Christian teaching helps. Even at an early age, five or six, God is working within us. Maybe because of a lack of distractions, each experience makes a deeper impression on young. The Holy Spirit is within us from the beginning of life. When we are young we are more receptive. The key word is receptive. With some, this word never finds a home.

God will love and take care of you regardless of your acceptance of Him. However, God will accept you only when you accept Him as the Lord of your life. That's right. The first move is yours. You don't have forever. He has granted you a limited amount of time to make the most important decision in your life. No decision is the same as a negative decision. The goal is to become a winner. You can't sit on the side lines and be considered a winner. Life is not a game. It's for real. There is no such thing as a draw. You either win or lose. Make your choice.

This Too Shall Pass

This Too Shall Pass

Why do you think people support evil people? Evil people who state that most people don't deserve respect. Evil people who with intent hurt others. People who have shown over and over again that they care about only me, myself, and I. Evil people who seek power and control for self-purposes. These kinds of people are in great numbers. They have great support. Why? Most people do not care about right or wrong. Most people have only the concern that they personally are not the subject of wrong.

Why does God permit these kinds of people to hurt others and control? It's a wake-up call. We want to think the best of people. The fact is, most people you meet every day will do anything they can get away with. What you see is not what you get. When it comes to a choice between them and you, you will come in second most of the time.

There are 155 countries on this earth. 145 of them do not believe in God and Jesus Christ. Most people you meet every day do not attempt to live their lives under the government of God. With most people, the name of God or Jesus does not cross their minds most days. You are in the minority in more ways than you think. Accept this fact. Most people will not go to heaven. In Hades there will be standing room only. But not in heaven. The ticket to heaven is expensive. You must pay the price. A lot of work is required. Both personal and non-personal work.

Often times we must live under the immediate control of evil people. We can only be thankful that this too shall pass. Hold on to God's unchanging hand. God will direct your path.

I Don't Know

I DON'T KNOW

Reading the bible can be confusing. One Scripture can have different meanings to different people. Any one Scripture can have more than one meaning. Understanding content is important to correct Scripture understanding. Often times the writer is talking about one particular set of circumstances. The statement might not apply to all situations.

Do you believe that only those people who accept Jesus Christ as the Son of God will go to heaven? If your answer is yes and you are correct, over 60% of the population of this world will go to Hades. Jesus stated that no one will go to the Father but by Him. Is He stating that if you do not believe in Him, you will not go to heaven? Or, is He simply stating that only He will make the decision? There are a lot of good people who could but do not go to church. Good people who live a righteous life. Who don't start no stuff. Who care about others and try to help others. Yet, have not orally committed to Jesus. Will these people be sent to Hades?

You cannot live a life without giving God the Glory and expect Him to glorify you. Are these people really disregarding God if they are living a life that basically would be pleasing in God's sight? Jesus forgave Paul because of his disbelief and ignorance. We serve a just God. Remember God's statement, He will have mercy on who He will have mercy.

When you get to heaven, the only person you should be surprised to see is yourself.

Believe In Jesus

We believe what we want to believe. There are 155 countries on this earth. 145 do not believe in Jesus. This is nothing new. When Jesus walked this earth, most people did not believe in Him. They numerous times wanted to stone Him to death. He told them, if you do not believe in me, believe in the miracles. He made people who could not walk, walk again. He made people who could not see, see again. He gave life to people who had died. Numerous times they wanted to stone Him to death. He did, many good works. He asked them for which of those works do you stone me? The Jews answered Him, saying. For a good work we stone thee not, but for blasphemy; and because that thou, being a man, makest thyself God.

We believe what we want to believe. We refuse to recognize that which is reasonable because it does not support that which we believe. The Jews knew that no man could perform the miracles performed by Jesus. They knew that His powers could have come only from God. They did not want to believe in Jesus. So they gave the obvious no consideration.

Sixty percent of the people alive on this earth today do not believe in Jesus or do not care one way or the other. This is where the blasphemy comes in. I believe in God because I want to believe in God. I believe in Jesus because I want to believe in Jesus. I believe in eternity because I want to believe. Let's be honest. We are selfish people. We are always thinking about ourselves. We don't want to believe that death is the end. We want to believe that our Souls will be saved. That we and our love ones will meet again. That after we leave this world, we will live forever with God Almighty.

Yes, we have some work to do on the reason we believe. But, we are more than half way there.
BELIEVE IN JESUS

Pain

There are more kinds of pain than can be written. From my head is hurting to I will never be able to get out of this bed under my own power alive. There are some pains that medication cannot help. Your doctor will ask you the level of your pain from one to ten. When you tell him/her the number eleven, it is time to turn to God. When you turn to God, you must know what to expect. We read in the bible where Jesus healed all kinds of human illness. These acts were miracles. Yes, He could perform a miracle for you, but, the miracle might not be what you are expecting.

Time will effectively lessen some forms of pain. It helps us in our subconscious effort. Our willingness to accept that which has happened to us. It is like you are in a dark room at night time. There is only one crack in the wall that is not obvious in the dark. Then daylight approaches and a beam of light breaks through that one crack. You start to understand that God is in control and when God is in control nothing can be out of control. Your level of hope and even comfort increases. You are better able to manage your situation. It still hurts. The pain is still there, but, your God is there too.

That's the miracle. The Holy Spirit is the miracle. You will develop to the point of being able to dance in the rain because your love for God is greater than anything that can happen to you here on this earth. You feel like Jesus. He suffered because His love for His Father was greater than His pain. You will be told that the ways of God are complex. No, they are not. The ways of God are very easy to accept when you accept the fact that God loves you.

Jesus told us these things so that in Him we may have peace. He said in this world we will have trouble. But take heart! Jesus has overcome the world.

Take heart. Your love for God is greater than anything that can happen to you in this world. Greater even than pain. When you hurt, don't think about the hurt, think about God. He will safely carry you through.

Image

For most of us, appearance is important. We want to look good. When people think of us, we want them to think of how we look and our financial status. We need to realize that our image to others have little to do with the material. When people think of you, the first thing that comes into their minds is the kind of person you are. Your character. When they put you in the ground, little to nothing will be said about your financial means or personal appearance.

Character is of primary importance. He/she was a good person. A God fearing person. Wouldn't you like that? People saying that you were a person who really Loved God. We can make this happen through our efforts to be more and more like Jesus every day. God made this possible. He created us in His likeness. "Let us make man in our likeness." (Genesis 1:26) What does this mean, in our likeness? Do you think you physically look like God? God is Spirit. He is thinking in the immaterial sense. He made us mentally, morally, and socially in His likeness. Because of this, we are rational volitional agents. We are reflections of God's holiness. We know when we are not doing the right thing. Guilt, like fear, can be a blessing. God wants us to have a freedom of choice. He will not force you to do anything. He will not force you to come to Him. Some humans make the wrong choice. Jesus will see that they pay for their actions.

God has given Jesus the power and authority to make the decision, heaven or hades. God has made it very simple for us. Do it My way and you will live happy ever after. He sent Jesus so that we would not make any mistakes. By following the Shepherd we become creations in the likeness of God. It's an easy choice. Your way or God's way. If you pick the wrong way, you have no one to blame but yourself. By the way, Jesus knows your heart. You can't fool Him. You can go to church, sing pretty songs of praise, and show all kinds of physical emotion. But if your heart and actions are not right, come judgment day, you will hear the words I never knew you. Simply because you never knew His Father.

Jesus

There are 155 countries on the face of the earth. 90% of Christians reside in only ten of them. These are considered Christian countries. 145 out of 155 countries do not believe in Jesus. 60% of the people in this world either do not believe in Jesus or could not care less. The fight of Jesus, Peter, Paul and many others is far from over.

Even most Christians fail to understand the full impact of Jesus. They think that the life of Jesus started with His birth into this world. God sent Jesus into this world to help us. God did not create Jesus for us. Jesus was with God far before the earth was formed. Read Scripture. It reads, God created all in five days. On the 6th day, man was created. Scripture reads, "Let us create man in our own likeness." (Genesis 1:26) Why are the words 'us' and 'our' used? 'Us' and 'our' could only mean that someone else was present. Jesus told us that He was with God from the beginning. God gave the instructions. Jesus carried them out.

We need to stop under estimating the capacity of Jesus. He told us that He had the power to give His life and the power to take it back. God did not force Jesus to go through the suffering that He endured. It was the decision of Jesus. He endured the pain and suffering because it was the Will of God.

60% of the people in this world still do not believe in Jesus. 60% of the people now on the face of the earth will go to Hades. That is not the number you want to be part of.

Believe in Me and I will be worthy of you.

Love

Love is a very important word. Like emotion, it can sometimes be only temporary. Only fifty percent of marriages are successful. This is because there are other things more important to some people than love. One would think that the love of one's mother and father would be the ultimate love. Love of the person who gave you birth. Love of the person who took care of you when you could not take care of yourself. Yet, there have been numerous reports of children murdering their parents. When is love really love? How easy it is to fall into and out of love. Humans fall into and out of love with each other with regularity. Emotion is a good thing, but, it is only temporary. We witness emotion in church, however, it only last for a short period of time. Love cannot last if the foundation is emotion.

Humans are not like God. They do not always mean what they say. They might think they do at the time, but, how deep is your love? No greater love has a friend than to give his/her life for another. This kind of love is rare. God gave His human life for love of us. Abraham was willing to give up his only son upon the request of God. How deep is your love? Only when nothing on the face of the earth can stand in the way is your love deep enough.

Human love for one another is not the same as love for God. Jesus has told us that God must come first. Love for Him must be greater than love for wife, child, parents, all. We might rarely be tested to determine if this is true. We might never be put in the same situation as Abraham, but, God knows our hearts. You do not fall in love with God. His love grows on you. Once you have it, you can never fall out of love with and for God. There is nothing in this world more important. Not even life itself. For it's not just for what you are Yourself that I love You as I do, but, for what I am when I am with You. He does something to you and for you. With His presence comes peace and hope. You feel that He is in control of your life and when God is in control nothing can be out of control. You can never fall out of love with your God. You can fall out of love with any human being, but, never with God because you know that His love is everlasting and His truth endureth forever. You can never fall out of love for Him because you know that He can never fall out of love for you. Regardless of what He puts your through, you know that it is out of love.

Can you imagine how much I love you? His love for you takes a strong imagination. I will forever live my life with love for my Heavenly Father. My God.

The Long Way Home

We believe in God and His Son Jesus the Christ. We have accepted Jesus as our Savior. We try to live our lives in a matter that is pleasing in the sight of God. There is only one question. Why? Why is this race so hard to run? Why the test when we try to do our best? God, what more do you want from me? I know He loves me. I can't understand why he has lead me down this path.

The Israelites also could not understand. After God freed them from slavery in Egypt, He did not give them an easy path to the Promise Land. The road was treacherous. He knew that they would want to take the easy way out. He knew that when times got hard, many would want to turn back. Give up. When times got hard, many rebelled. Many sinned. Their faith was weak and lead them to forty years of wandering in a dry land. Only when the next generation trusted in their God, could they see the finish line. Only when the Israelites understood that they were not capable of understanding God, could their dreams be fulfilled.

We want to see the land of Milk and Honey as much as the Israelites. God knows the directions to the Promise Land. Only when we understand that we are not capable of understanding and are willing to follow the path directed by our Heavenly Father without question, will we arrive at Jericho and the walls will come tumbling down.

The finish line is really all that matters. Making it to the finish line. Nobody said the road would be easy, but, I don't believe He brought me this far to leave me.

The Battle

The Battle

Satan will always be at the door waiting for you to fall, waiting for you to be less than you could be should be. Jesus has given us the Victory. Satan knows he is a loser, but, he is also a die hard. He wants to keep everyone possible from enjoying the Victory. Satan was formerly an angel. Lucifer was an archangel. A leader of other angels. He got some angels to follow him instead of following God. They tried to take over God's kingdom. God put them out of heaven. They landed on earth and have been raising sin ever since.

Satan has his limitations. The Victory that Jesus gave us includes control of the devil. Satan can only do what we permit him to do. The angels that followed him are now call demons. They still work for the devil. They are the reason Lucifer can be in so many places at the same time. They remain active in our lives but under our control.

We are in a unique position. How would you like to play in a basketball game that you already know you have won? That is what the Victory of Jesus means to us. We live our lives wearing the armor of Jesus. Satan is helpless. He will not give up. Temptation is his weapon. He will keep trying to penetrate the armor of Jesus forever. But he cannot win unless you let him win. When he comes knocking, laugh at him. Why is he coming after you so hard? Because you are a threat to him. You are rubbing salt in his memory of his rejection when he attempted temptation upon Jesus. The only thing that we as God's people have to be careful about is not being careful. We cannot permit Lucifer to even think that there might be a crack in the armor we are wearing. One hole and he will find new life. His methods of temptation are tricky. He knows that we are weak. He knows that only Jesus is keeping him from accomplishing his mission. There is nothing that he will not try. He is also thinking, what will it take to get you? It could be something little or big. He won't go away. Keep plenty of oil for your lamp. You never know when he might come.

Rounding Third And Headed For Home

Rounding Third And Headed For Home

Heaven is a prepared place for prepared people. You become prepared by having faith in God. Only people with wisdom enough to accept God at His word will be prepared to accept His wisdom because wisdom is dependent upon faith. How deep is your faith? Words are cheap. Anyone can stand the test for a short period of time. True faith is dependent upon confidence and patients. Wisdom to understand that God is in control. He will make the decisions as to timing. True wisdom demands confidence that He will deliver using His time table. Wait on the Lord. True wisdom depends on faith and true faith depends on confidence in God and patients.

Prosperity is a misunderstood word. It has nothing to do with that which is material. You can be prosperous without the big house and luxury car. Scripture states that Joseph was prosperous even as a slave because he had the wisdom of God. Knowing God is what makes us prosperous. This joy I have, the world didn't give it and the world can't take it away. It is so obvious once we think it out. There is a reason for coming into this world with nothing and leaving with nothing. Nothing minus nothing equals nothing. We have two hearts. One that keeps us alive and one that is the reason for living. It is so obvious once we think it out. The important heart is the one that directs us to God. That heart and soul can be touched by man only if we allow. God gave us the authority to makes all decisions and have complete control over the important heart and our souls. Nothing can have an effect on either without our permission.

When our name is called, the condition of our heart and soul will be the determining points. God does not determine if you will join Him and His Son in heaven. You do. God does not determine if you are saved. You do. He has given you complete control. He has given you all the tools needed to ensure that when you reach the stage in life of rounding third, you will be saved at home.

It is so obvious once we think it out.

Proclaiming The Gospel Of Jesus Christ

Christianity is the largest faith on the face of the earth. The Muslim faith is a distant second. 90% of Christians reside in only ten countries. These are considered Christian Nations. The other ten percent of Christians reside in countries that do not necessarily tolerate Christianity. Many of those Christians fear daily for their lives. 145 out of 155 countries on the face of this earth do not believe in Jesus. Jesus said no one comes to the Father but by Me. Yet, the pastor of the largest Christian congregation in America will not state that Jesus is the only road to God. Even he gives Jesus only 90% support. Yet, there would be no Christianity were it not for Jesus. 60% of the people in this world do not believe that Jesus is the Son of God. Six out of ten people on the average that you meet every day either do not believe in Jesus or could not care less one way other the other.

The fight of Jesus, Peter, Paul, and thousands of others is not over. Jesus said that we will be hated by people in this world because of Him. This is still true two thousand years later. Christianity is in the minority in this world. Christianity is under attack even today. Jesus has given us His support. We have an obligation to give Him our support. Talk is cheap. We must stand up and be counted. We must be of the mind set of saving one soul at a time. The only way that you will succeed is to let it be known that you are a Christian because of what Jesus has done in your life. Not every person who states to be a Christian will go to heaven. Don't be one of those Christians who never make it to heaven. Yes, God has stated that He will have mercy on whom He will have mercy. But, we must live by the rule not by the exception to the rule. Do you want to make it to heaven? Bless some one's life. You want to make it to heaven. Keep Jesus in your mind every day. You want to make it to heaven. Keep growing in the Spirit of Jesus.

Grace And Mercy

Grace And Mercy

GRACE is receiving something that we do not deserve. Mercy is not receiving something that we do deserve. The silly games that people play. Never meaning what they say and they don't say what they mean. Till they are covered up with flowers in the back of a black limousine. Jesus hated the actions of hypocrites. In His day, He was talking about Sadducees and Pharisees. He hated their actions primarily because "You shut the kingdom of heaven in men's faces. You yourselves do not enter, nor will you let those enter who are trying to." (Matthew 23:13) People who never live the life they talk about. Some things change. Some things never change. There are hypocrites with us today. There are degrees of hypocrisy. The pretense of having feelings or characterizes one does not possess.

People who call themselves Christians. Who hide behind the Cross of Jesus Christ. Never meaning what they say and they don't say what they mean. This is the worst degree of hypocrisy. A friend of mine told me about a preacher who would not take care of his sick wife. He would not give to her medication or feed her properly. He would be in church Sunday morning delivering his sermon while his wife was home in bed lying in her own body waste. His statement was, the Lord will provide. He will surely go to Hades. You might fool some of the people, but, you can never fool God.

There are good people who try to do the right things, but, have not accepted God and Jesus into their lives. There are those who believe in both God and Jesus, but, have not declared Their greatest. These people do not think daily about God's grace and mercy. The Souls of these people are completely dependent upon God's mercy. Not receiving something that they deserve. God will have mercy on whom He will have mercy. We all sin, but, one of the greatest sins we can commit is not accepting God into our lives. Mercy alone is living by the exception. Christians must live by the rules of God not by the exception to the rule.

We must pray that our Souls will receive the Grace of God. Something that we do not deserve. We will all need His mercy, but, we can only be Saved by the Grace of God.

Why Jesus

God has tried many ways to get His message to humanity. He tried prophets, judges, and kings. Nothing worked to the degree of His desire. A decision had to be made. Either give up on humanity or sacrifice all. God loves us too much to ever give up. He made His decision. "The Word became flesh and made his dwelling among us" (John 1:14) The reason that Jesus was born a Jew is because God knew He would receive resistance. There is a difference between a lack of believe and unbelieve. The Jewish people suffered from a combination of the two. Their biggest problem was that they wanted God to be what they wanted Him to be instead of becoming what God wanted them to become. They suffered from both natural and voluntary sin. They knew that Jesus was not an ordinary man, but, they cared more about their positions among the people than the Will of God.

Some things change. Some things never change. Sixty percent of the people alive on the face of the earth today do not believe in Jesus. Do not believe that Jesus is the Son of God. Even after all of His suffering and sacrifices, most still do not believe. Most will never believe. This is a life of choices. You believe what you want to believe. The choices of people do not come without consequences. God will judge those who are mentally able to distinguish between good and evil. Believe it or not, the choice between the acceptance of Jesus and some other way is a choice between good and evil. There are those who believe there is another road to God other than by Jesus. They reason, how can God not accept these people who are on their knees with their heads to the ground daily praying to Him. The question should be, how can such people not accept He who suffered and died for their sins? How could they not accept the Son of God? Again, people who want God to be what they want Him to be instead of becoming what God wants them to be.

There are Christians and Jews who believe there is a road to God other than Jesus Christ. There are Christian preachers who will preach for an hour and the name Jesus never comes out of their mouths. There are Jews who claim to believe in the Jewish Jesus, who believe He is only another road to the Kingdom of God.

God has done all He can do to let you know His love. He tried prophets, judges, kings. He sent His Son to deliver the message. Jesus said while on the Cross, "it is finished". (John 19:30) It is finished. God will not force you to believe in Him and in Jesus. It is finished. God has done His part. Now you must do your part. You have to only ask, Jesus Come into My Life.

The Preacher Said

There are a few things of which we Christians should mentally make adjustments. One most important is the understanding that God inspires man God does not perfect man. Every human being who has lived has made mistakes. That includes writers of scripture and preachers. It is hard to come to terms with. We so badly want to believe that every word in the bible is exactly as spoken. We do not want to believe that man had a negative influence on scripture. We understand that many of the writers of scripture could only report that which they were told having no way to determine the accuracy of the information. We understand that the translators of scripture into English had the opportunity to add their own opinions without being detected. Yet, we want to believe that scripture is word perfect. We believe what we want to believe.

A preacher was asked, how were people Saved before Jesus? His answer was that all people are sinners and all people went to their grave upon death. With the Resurrection of Jesus, all who were good rose to receive eternal life. He could be right. We believe what we want to believe. Others believe that the birth of Jesus into this world was not the birth of Jesus into existence. Jesus was with God far before the creation of heaven and earth. Jesus was doing God's work far before we knew about Him. Abraham, Noah, Moses, Job and many others were, upon their deaths, judged by Jesus and found their place in God's Kingdom to continue serving God. We believe what we want to believe.

A preacher said, on the Cross Jesus cried out "Eloi Eloi, Iama sabachtani" meaning "My God, my God, why have you forsaken me?"(Matthew 27:45) By forsaking Jesus, God would never have to forsake man. The preacher could be right. Read the gospel of John. John was there at the foot of the Cross. Jesus spoke directly to John. John heard every word that was spoken by Jesus. Nowhere in the gospel of John will we find any indication that Jesus questioned understanding of God's devotion to Him. We believe what we want to believe.

Do we believe in the writings of man more than we believe in the Divine Nature of Jesus? NO, Jesus, the Son of God, He who was at the right hand of the Almighty before the creation of heaven and earth, could have never, not even in His most trying moments, spoken such words. God could never forsake Jesus and Jesus could never doubt His Father. It is all in what you believe.

Believe in God, Jesus, and the Holy Ghost. Nothing else is perfect. Nothing.

Anti-Semitism

Why is it that we never hear the word used with any group of people other than Jews? Jews are the most hated group of people in the world. Every twenty-five years somewhere they have been subject to persecution, discrimination, and/or expulsion. Jews have historically had a bad reputation. They developed a strong financial foundation by focusing on financial control because they were not permitted to own land. They developed a reputation as loan sharks. There is nothing that Jews have done that other groups could not have done. Now they, a small percentage of the world's population, have a powerful financial dominance. Success in areas such as marketing, technology, media, industry, cinema. Jewish money has meaningful control in the United States through companies like Ralph Lauren, Levis, Calvin Klein, Dell computers, Oracle, Google and Facebook. ABC, CBS, and NBC have Jewish entrepreneur connections. As a result, it is estimated that ninety percent of Jews in the U.S. are rich.

Is it true that Jews have an attitude? Could it be that Jews believe that they are God's chosen people and regardless of their small numbers they will continue to overcome and control. Do they deep within believe that they have a higher moral standard than others? Most members of the Jewish faith are born Jews. It's a family affair. They will not admit that they are the reason Christ Jesus was crucified. They will not accept responsibility for His death. Most Jews do not believe in His Resurrection. Some have changed. Some do now believe that Jesus is the Son of God. However, these same people also believe that Jesus is not the only road to the Father. If Jews do not repent, that inside track that they believe they have with God might not be leading to heaven.

The Easy Way Out

Sure I believe in God and Jesus. What have I to lose? If I am right. I go to heaven. If I am wrong, I'm back where I started. You will see these people in church on Easter Sunday only. These are what is known as strategy Christians. They are in for a big surprise when they hear Jesus tell them, I never knew you. Jesus came to us for Spiritual and social reasons. When we only occupy ourselves with the spiritual, we ignore over thirty years of the life of our Savior. His liberating actions do not become a standard for Christian actions. To focus only on the Resurrection, without the entire ministry of Jesus, is to do harm and injustice to the Good News of the gospel. There is no easy way out if you are to be a sincere Christian.

Sharing the gospel not only means bible study but life involvement. We as Christians should be outspoken not meek and passive. We are to speak out in the name of Jesus. Christians are the disciples and apostles of Christ today. Sharing the gospel is our duty. You are not fooling God by being a meek passive Christian. What good is it if a person claims to have faith but has no deeds? Stop being a strategy Christian. God don't play that.

Love Your Enemy

When reading the bible, we must understand that traditions of the Jewish people had a major effect upon that which was written. Slavery was a Jewish tradition during the time scripture was written. Therefore, with this understanding, we cannot relate all that is written in the bible to be acceptable in our society. Love thy neighbor. Jews did not consider everyone their neighbor. They considered only Jews to be neighbors. Jesus was not a Christian. He was a Jewish Rabbi. A Jew who tried to change Jewish tradition and bring understanding to the way Jews had been thinking for hundreds of years. Many Jews did not take the change well. They considered Jesus their enemy. One who harbors malicious intent toward them. They considered Jesus a hostile power who had to be silenced.

Jesus wanted Jews to understand that God's way was not their way. That one's neighbor was not just of like kind, but, all of God's creations. Even one's enemy. Because a person does not agree with your ways and belief, does not make that person less of a child of God. We might not like a person, but, Jesus is telling us to still show that person God's love.

You are not Jesus. The Holy Spirit is not finish with you yet. You are still growing in the Spirit. Jesus is not telling us to help people who will continue to bring harm to others. He is not telling us to do good to evil people. Jesus ask God to forgive those who were taking His life because they know not what they do. He did not say condone their actions. In showing God's love to our enemy, we imitate God.

Good (vs) Bad

This battle will continue to go on until the return of Jesus. There are some people who have no respect for others. The law is the only thing that keeps some of them in line. Wild human animals. There are many reasons for the way they have become. The way they were raised could be one reason. Products of their childhood teaching or lack of teaching. Many are too weak to live life the right way. It takes effort to live God's way. We have to accept the fact that we are living in a world of fools stepping on dreams. People like this use fear as their weapon. Fear is not always bad. It shows respect for God's position in our lives. We should not fear anyone who can take our lives. We should fear He who can take our lives and our souls.

Protect yourself from Satan. He is all around. A master of dissuasion. You have the responsibility to stay around in a condition that will permit you to help God's people. That is the reason God is keeping you here. You will be around to give God your best only if you work hard and smart. Change the world one person at a time. When you change one person's life, you have changed the world.

Control

There is nothing more powerful in this world than control. Everyone is under the control of something or someone. The reason people do what they do is because of beliefs. We should all want to believe that God is in control of everything that happens here on earth. When bad things happen, did God make them happen, did God permit them to happen? I am one who will not believe that God kills innocent people. People who are doing no wrong to anyone. I do not understand it, but, I do believe that I serve a God of love and mercy. God controls that which He wants to control. He has a reason for permitting bad things to happen to good people. I do not know His reason. I can and will only trust in Him.

There is one fact that Christians should be sure of. They will never understand God. Without understanding, they cannot defend the actions of God. God does not want you to be able to prove His existence. God does not want you to be able to defend His actions. God does not want you to have complete understanding of Him. God is beyond all of these things. God is above all of these things. God is the beginning and the end. He does whatever He wants to do and for good reason. Our lack of understanding does not change this fact. He is God all by Himself. No one and nothing is the reason for His being. He is capable of controlling all things. We want Him to control our lives for nothing can be out of control when God is in control.

Communication

The Lord is demanding. He requires a certain standard be maintained by His children. When that standard is not to His satisfaction, He has a history of discipline. One takes disciplinary action justly when there is love. If God had no love for His children, He would not care what they did. God often gives us numerous opportunities to straighten up and fly right. Some of us have wisdom enough to take advantage of His offer, some don't.

In early times, God communicated through His prophets. Isaiah, Samuel, Ezekiel, Jeremiah, and Daniel tried to let the Israelites know God's Will. Later, God sent Jesus. Jesus came to give understanding to the message given by the prophets. Jesus knew that the line of communication between God and His people had to continue after He left earth. The Holy Spirit was His way of making sure the communication between God and His people would never end. Prayer is communication with God through the Holy Spirit. Only if we are willing to listen to God's word will His communication with us be fruitful. God has pulled out all the stops. He has spoken to us in many ways. We must listen or we will find that our lives are useless. Without purpose. We must love Him sincerely with all our heart, soul, mind, and strength or we will go to Hades. It is just that simple. There is nothing in between. If you don't believe me, you can find out the hard way.

The Devil Made Me Do It

THE DEVIL MADE ME DO IT

God told the children of Israel that they would be given the land of milk and honey. The problem was the land belonged to another people. When we are told something by the Holy Spirit, we have a decision to make. Believe it and go through whatever it takes to make it happen or decide there must be something wrong with the decision of God. The decision to accept the command of God and to go through whatever it takes can sometimes put us in a tight spot. God specializes in tight spots. You might be called into battle many times, but, always remember God takes care of His people.

That is what it takes to find your way to Paradise. Jesus said that He will return in the Glory of God, with the angels of God, to reward us for what we have done in this life. This tells us, that we will receive benefit for the good that we do in this life. When will we receive the reward Jesus has promised? After we get to heaven. Everyone will be rewarded to the degree that is deserved. All will not be equal in Paradise. Those who have done more to promote the Kingdom of God will receive more JOY when we are at home with our Father. Helping people is what Jesus was all about. Helping others is what we should be all about.

Holy Spirit

Divine Revelation. The manifestation of a mystical communication from a supernatural Divine source. Jesus breathed on His disciples for them to receive the Holy Spirit. God communicates with us by way of the Holy Spirit. God will forever communicate with us if we are willing to listen. Not everyone is ready to receive the Holy Spirit. You must be willing to obey and permit God to take control of your life. You must give up all control of your life to Him. When this happens, you will receive communication from God by means of Divine Revelation. You will not be perfect. You have come to the realization that this is God's world. He will help you overcome. He has prepared a better more Divine place for you. You will come to the realization that whatever happens to you on this earth is secondary to your life with Him in heaven.

The Holy Spirit sets its own rules. It can come to you any place and any time. It has no age limitations. When a child six years of age on his sick bed ask his daddy to pray with him, you know this is true. We see the reaction to the Holy Spirit often times in church. Some people jump and shout. Some just pat their foot. Others cry tears of joy. There is nothing more precious to us than our love for God. We are not born Saved. We must pray and ask God to Save us.

Jesus found something worth dying for, you. Now it is your turn to live for God.

Pain II

There is both physical and emotional pain. Often times physical pain brings on emotional pain. Sometimes, emotional pain will bring on physical pain. We seem to concentrate more on physical pain. Most medications are to help relieve physical pain. The New Testament seems to deal more with the healing of the body than of the heart and mind. Emotional pain can come from numerous directions. Many times, there is nothing that a pill or shot can correct. Emotional pain can be serious. It can drive a person to alcohol or drugs. It has even driven people to suicide. We often wonder why emotional pain is not directly addressed in scripture. We sometimes have to read between the lines to find it.

Is God emotional? Scripture tells us that Jesus was at times emotional. Jesus wept. Showing sorrow is emotional. Showing love is also emotional. Jesus loved Martha and her sister of Lazarus. Simon son of John, do you love me. You will love your God with all you heart, soul, and mind. The emotion we sometimes see in church does not last very long. True love will be displayed through doing. Peter showed his love for Jesus by living the remainder of his life serving Jesus. The Beatitudes are statements of emotion. The Beatitudes address those who are poor in spirit. We are also told to rejoice. God wants to make us feel good both physically and mentally.

Both physical and mental application require deep belief in God. You will not see the lame walk or other miracles happen, but, God is daily working on our minds as well as our bodies. This is important because our minds are more important than our bodies. Our minds are under the control of our hearts. When we give our hearts to Jesus, He controls our minds even if our bodies are limited. There are some who are still walking around dead. Spiritually dead. We can only pray for them. We who believe are blessed with the Spirit of God in our hearts. Confessing with your mouth is not enough. God will see if the Holy Spirit is truly working within your heart controlling your mind and your body, your actions. We can control all things, even pain, through the power of God.

Ransom

Jesus spoke direct so that there could be no mistakes. Jesus stated that He came to give His life as a ransom for many. Payment in full. Jesus paid the required price to set us free from sin. Until the love of Jesus was shown on the Cross, we were slaves to sin, but, now we are released from sin and reconciled with God. Never again can anything separate us from the love of God. Not even fear. Fear can control a person's actions. Fear is based on facts. Faith is based on Spirit. Our faith in God and Jesus overrides fear through the Holy Spirit. The Holy Spirit is part of the gift given us through the ransom paid by Jesus. So often, we face hardships that are out of our control. We can do absolutely nothing to make things better. They are not battles. We can fight a battle. We cannot fight a storm. When storms keep blowing in your life, your soul must be anchored in the Lord. You can only hope to survive. Out last the storm. The ransom Jesus paid makes this possible. He said, I will be with you always even until the end of the world. We only have to call on Him to outlast the storm. He will be our shield. Only because of His ransom will we be able to survive every storm. God has commended time to console the unhappy.

Our faith will be put to the test. We often wonder, why. We understand that we were not meant to understand. Nothing will turn the love of God from us and nothing will turn our love for God. The Lord giveth and the Lord taketh away. Blessed be the name of the Lord. I will trust in the Lord till I die. The storms may keep blowing in my life, but, because of the ransom of Jesus, my soul has been anchored in the Lord.

Boss

Boss

Most of us do not like the word boss. We do not even like the word when it is used to describe us. We will accept the word only when it has attached benefits. Don't tell me what to do unless you are going to compensate me for doing it. A boss who is free hearted is more acceptable. Most people who are in the position of boss, are free hearted only if you are willing to accept their authority. Most people in authority will permit a limited number of errors. However, they do have limits because their primary interest is not you. It is the success of the company. Many people are insane. Insanity is doing the same thing the same way over and over again and expecting different results. We don't like change. Many times we must be forced into it. We are fixed on repetition. We even sit in the same place when we go to church. Repetition of sin can lead to bondage.

We can, through repetition, develop an innate desire to sin making it more difficult to fight temptation. This is a part of our human nature. Stay around the wrong people long enough and you will start acting like them. It is difficult for us to forgive the wrong of another. Scripture tells us to forgive four hundred and forty times nine. It follows by stating, or as many times as asked. We are blessed that there is no limit to the forgiveness of God. But, we must ask. If you do not sincerely seek His forgiveness, you will not receive it. We might be repeat offenders, but, insanity does not apply to God.

God is the Boss. God permitted your life and has told you exactly how He wants you to live it. He brought you into this world and He will take you out. He will reward you for following His commands. The ultimate reward is a place with Him for eternity. Repetition can be good. It can create habits that please the Lord. God has made you numerous promises here in this life and in the hereafter. These promises are actually payments for your goodness. You don't receive a check in the mail once a week or once every two weeks. You get paid every day. There will also be a bonus day. A day that will be the most glorious day of your life. Hang in there. It will be worth it. If you get fired on your job, you can always find another job. The last thing you want to hear is the boss, God, saying you are fired. No mind has conceived what God has prepared for those who love Him.

I Owe You

Grace is being given something that you do not deserve. Something of value. Most Christians do not like to be in the debt of anyone. If someone walked up to you and just gave you a lot of money, you might accept it, but, deep inside you would not really like it. You would rather earn the money. That way you would not feel that you are in the debt of that person. Many Christians are the same way when the gift comes from God. We want to earn His grace. We want to earn Salvation.

Think about it. Our desire to earn turns God into a prostitute. He then would be paying you for your services. God don't play that. We wonder if God keeps score. We believe that He is a just God. Scripture tells us that He will not forget the good that we have done for His people and His kingdom. Surely God has some standards for His Grace. He will not just grant grace to anyone regardless of their actions. Or will He? We do not know what these standards are. Another mystery. What we do know is that we are not capable of thinking like God.

Jesus keeps score. He has said that He will return to give each person what they deserve for the good or bad that has have done while in this body. This reward can only be given after we are in heaven. It will not help us to get to heaven. Only the Grace of God will determine our entrance into His kingdom. We don't owe God anything. You cannot owe a debt that you can never repay. We must accept the gifts of God with a cheerful heart. Knowing that it is given out of His love. There is nothing wrong with wanting to give something back for His goodness. This is not repayment. It is a show of gratitude. We try to live our lives in a way that is hopefully pleasing in God's sight because we want Him to know that we love and appreciate Him. Thank you for Your love. Thank you for Your goodness. Thank you for Your Grace that has carried me through. I will continue to live my life following Your Will and Your Way. I will continue to try to help others to understand Your place in their lives. Just because I love YOU.

A Gift From God

Scripture tells us that faith is being sure of what we hope for and certain of what we do not see. This is telling us that faith is invisible. It is something we visualize on the inside that is not manifest on the outside. Inner direction. We walk by faith not by sight. Faith determines our direction in life. We are following something that is invisible to the eye, yet, we see it clearly. We have the ability to see the invisible. Evidence of things unseen. You cannot see or touch it, but, you know it is there. Often times common sense tells you not to believe because faith makes no sense. There are many questions for which life provides no answers. Sometime you have to believe in miracles. You have no proof, yet, you still believe.

Our faith can grow weary. Because faith is intangible, we have nothing that we can physically hold on to, we sometimes waver. We waver because we have lost contact with God. We might continue to go through the motions doing the bare minimum. But we have lost contact with God. It is at these times that you are truly blessed because even when your faith in God wavers, God's faith in you remains firm. Therefore, being justified by faith, we have peace with God through our Lord Jesus Christ.

Jesus. You have never seen Him. You have to believe in miracles to believe He is real. You have to believe in miracles to believe, after dying on the Cross, He lives. He lives. My Saviour lives. The Redeemer of my Soul. I know He lives. He lives in my heart. In God, in Jesus, my Faith will never grow weary.

Understanding

There are many things in life that we do not understand. We do not understand God. His ways are not our ways. Faith is not a positioning response from God. Faith moves us to receive the peace of God. Faith gives us the courage to stay on the battlefield for our Lord without full understanding. Courage is nothing more than fear that has said its prayers. We are like lambs, a young sheep, following the Shepherd. Not knowing, we would not if we might, for it is better to walk with God in the darkness than walk alone in the light. Our Shepherd is Jesus. We don't need superstars. We have a hero role-model by which to direct our lives. Jesus, sent by our Heavenly Father to show us the way to the Promised Land. We must remember our place our role in this story. We must remember that every saint has a past and every sinner has a future. We must continue to fight a good fight. More important is the reason for the fight. Our reason for living. By serving God, we live life more abundantly.

We too often judge others on their actions while judging ourselves on our intentions. Simply because we do not understand others. The laws of man are for wrongdoers. Not for us. We live under the government of God. We don't need man's laws to govern our lives. We will not kill, steal, or hurt others because God controls our behavior even when times are difficult. We do not understand why difficult people are placed in our lives. Vultures and Ravens are considered dirty birds. Yet, God has used Ravens to serve His will. Ravens have been used to carry food to God's people who could not feed themselves. We must understand, when difficult people enter your life, that God is using these people, just as He used the Ravens, to help us grow in His Spirit. Handle each situation with God's gloves.

We often do not understand the love of God. Why does He permit bad things to happen to good people? If God loves me, why does He not give me all of His blessings now instead of withholding them from me? We remember the bible story of the young man who demanded that his father give him his inheritance immediately instead of withholding it. He was not mature enough to manger these gifts. God knows you better than you know yourself. God wants you to keep coming to Him seeking His blessings. God wants you to keep depending upon Him to direct your life. He know how much you can handle at each stage of life. Trust in His wisdom. Understand that there is no greater wisdom. Permit God to order your steps. Permit God to direct your life.

Who Are You?

You are a child of God. You have accepted Jesus as your Savior. You try to do right, but, sometimes you sin. You continue to hold your shortcomings over your head. When you were baptized, you were not made perfect. You are not a sinner because you sin. You sin because you are a sinner. You were born a sinner and there is nothing you can do to change it. You must first accept the fact that the Spirit of Jesus is within you. This will never change. You are born again. You will always come back to the Lord when you do the wrong thing. Repent means change. Understand that you have been placed on the right track to heaven. When you do wrong, that is not who you really are. You are undergoing a transformation into the person God wants you to be. It takes time to grow in the Spirit of God. Nothing this good can happen instantly. It takes time for the Holy Spirit to transform old bad habits into new good habits. Sooner or later, you will wonder why you have no desire to do that which you use to do. No desire to be around certain people you use to hang with. You can't explain it. It is God changing your life from the inside out. You are still a sinner and you will again do the wrong thing, but, you will always come back to God and seek His forgiveness. You will promise Him that you will try hard to change. To become the person He wants you to be. You have a new standard. His name is Jesus. He will help you fight your battle against sin. You will grow to enjoy the battle. It's you and Jesus against Satan. Satan will do everything possible to take you away from Jesus. But, you are a changed person. Nothing can separate you from the love of God and nothing can separate God from your love. The devil can go to Hades or some other hot place. Lucifer hates to come in second. He will keep coming after you every way he can because you are a threat to him. He is unable to take your Soul and he is afraid that you might make it difficult to take the Soul of another. He knows he has lost the war, but, he wants to keep as many as possible from enjoying the Victory of Jesus. He will keep throwing evil temptation after temptation at you, but, your Soul has been anchored in the Lord. Get thee behind me Satan. I am a child of God.

Faith dictates actions. The more faithful you are to the word of God, the better you will act in accordance to the word of God. The fact is that we are not all we should be. Our faithfulness is not always all it should be. If it were, we would not sin. Lord, help my lack of faith. When we think of death, regardless of how much faith we have, we still have our reservations because we are human. We believe that God will provide for us, but in the back of our minds, we still have a reservation that we cannot surrender. Faith does dictate actions, but, actions do not dictate our faith. We sometimes do and say things that do not indicate who we really are. We serve a faithful God. His faith is not like our faith. There are no degrees to the faith of God. Regardless of what we sometimes do or say, God's faith in us remains the same. Our actions do not indicate our faith in God. If it did, there would be highs and lows in our faith in God. Such is not the case. Our faith in God is not affected by our actions. That is true faith. Faith that God's faith will always be head and shoulders above our faith. Faith that our God will do everything He said He will do. There are many kinds of faith. Faith to discern, faith to persevere, obedient faith, disciplined faith. The most important faith is faith in God's faith. For only God's faith is perfect.

He Lives

Jesus suffered and died for all humanity. No greater love has one than to give his life for another. Jesus loved us before He died and He loves us now. The Resurrection of Jesus is the most wonderful event in our lives. It gives us joy. It has planted a seed within us that will grow and grow in the Spirit of God. Nothing can separate God from our love. We are sinners. We will sin. But, we will know we have done wrong and we will seek the Lord's forgiveness. Because of the Resurrection of Jesus, we are no longer what we use to be and we can never return to that level. We are filled with the Spirit of God. It feels so good to be a child of the Most High. It makes you feel like you are walking on air. Nothing is more important to you now. Not even life itself. You have to only close your eyes and give it all to Jesus. Free at last, free at last, thank God Almighty, I'm free at last.

Jesus suffered and died for us. He gave us His all. One would think that all the world would rejoice. It hurts to realize that 60% of the people in this world do not believe in Jesus. Christians have to wake-up and stop thinking that the world is on their side. On the side of Jesus. Six out of every ten people you meet, on an average, either do not believe in Jesus or could not care less one way or the other. There are 155 countries on the face of the earth. 145 out of 155 do not believe that Jesus the Christ is the Son of God. Christianity is under attack. It is true that Christianity is the largest faith in this world, but in total population, Christianity is in the minority. Jesus did all He could. It is finished. He has left the fight in our hands. It is our duty to save every Soul possible in the name of Jesus. We have to fight in the Spirit of Jesus, Peter, Paul, and thousands who have died and would die again for the love of God. A Love so strong that God gave His only Son to save His people.

Stay of the battlefield for our Lord. Not only in word, but, in LIFE.

Only Jesus

We sometimes read Scripture that would make one think that Jesus was less than Divine. Writings indicting that Jesus might have questionable faith in God. Asking why His Father had forsaken Him. Those who believe these written statements do not understand the Divine nature of Jesus the Christ. Jesus, like God, had no beginning. We are told in Scripture, by Jesus, that He was with God before the creation of the earth. Let US make man. The New Testament was translated from Greek. Monogens is the Greek word meaning generated. The only generated Son of God. Not created, generated. There are those who have been created by God. Adam and angels are examples of God's creations. They were physically created. Adam was physically not spiritually created. Jesus is the only begotten Son of God. Begotten meaning one and only. One of a Kind. Generated from the bosom of God. Having the Spirit of God. The Holy Spirit. No one could have the Holy Spirit of God other than Jesus until Jesus permitted them to have it. This Divine Spirit could never question God's faith in Him and He could never show any signs of a lack of faith in His Heavenly Father.

Christ means The Anointed One. After being baptized by John the Baptist, Jesus was taken to be with His Father. He was at that time anointed by the power of the Holy Spirit. Only Jesus had the power of God's Holy Spirit. No one could have this power while Jesus was on earth. Only Jesus could give this Power to them.

We are saved by the Grace of God. Saved means we are born again. We become born again when we believe in Jesus. We are born again when we understand that nothing we can do will help us get to heaven. Nothing we can do but believe in Jesus. Jesus is the image of the invisible God. When we see Jesus, we see God. We can see Jesus without ever looking into His face. It does not matter what He looks like physically. We know what He looks like inside. He looks like His Father. The Creator of Heaven and Earth. He stated, I and my Father are one. God said, this is My Son of whom I am well pleased.

Sacrifice

Father, Your Will not mind. I love the Lord. So often we make this statement. The question is, how much? There can be no love without sacrifice. The question is, do you want God's Will and Way to reign? To have supreme power. You go to church and sing pretty songs of praise. You pray. But, are you willing to stop doing that which God has told you not to do? You must prove your love. Love is not just words, but also actions. Your body is God's temple. When you do anything with your body that is not pleasing to God you have committed a sin. There is a sin without and a sin within. The greater sin is a sin within. Stealing something is a sin without. Shooting drugs, alcohol, homosexuality are sins within. They are greater sins because you are destroying God's temple in the process. Scripture tells us that having sex with a person of the same gender is detestable. Scripture states that if a man lies with a man as one lies with a woman, both of them have done what is detestable. They must be put to death; their blood will be on their own heads. Scripture does not state death for one who steals. A sin within is greater than a sin without. One must go to God and ask to be forgiven for all sins. Repentance means change. When you repent, you are stating that you will reframe from doing that which is against God's Will and Way. This will take sacrifice. You must put that which satisfies the body behind that which satisfies God. How strong is your love for God? Is your love for God so weak that you will permit momentary pleasure to overcome your love for God?

Man has a way of trying to make his wrong behavior look acceptable. He will say we changed the Sabbath Day to the first day of the week because of the Resurrection of Jesus. When the fact is that no human being has the authority to change a command of God. Homosexuals will say love of another is all that is important. When the fact is that the command of God is all that is important. Ask yourself, is your love for God greater than your love for earthly satisfaction? You might be fooling yourself, but, you are not fooling God. Repent, change. Ask God for the strength to change. He sent Jesus to help you correct your wayward way. The blood of Jesus has the power to wash away your unwished ways. Your unsteady capricious. Ask God for the help of Jesus. Show God that His Will and Way means more to you than anything in this world. Jesus made the supreme sacrifice for us out of love. Show God how much you love Him.

Saved

When you accept Jesus as your Savior and Lord, you are saved. You are, as of that moment in your life, blessed and highly favored. It is inside of you. You only have to bring it out. You must believe that God has given you all that you need to succeed in life. You lack nothing. You are God's choice. You have been Saved. You have not been made perfect. Inside, you have been made a new person. There are times when the old you will surface. There are times when you will sin. Your actions, at that time, are not who you are. You will continue to grow in God's Spirit until all that is old is put behind you. It is a process of renewing your mind in the Spirit of God. You have only to sincerely repent and keep on growing. You have been blessed with resilience. The ability to spring back and overcome all difficulties because you have the hand of God on your side. Nothing can stop you now for you are a child of God. You are Saved. The Spirit of Jesus is in you. When you pray, you are inviting the gifts of God to fill your heart and mind. You are praying for wisdom, strength and direction to set straight that which you can and to give to God that which only He can straighten. When you are Saved, you are granted a Spirit, heart, and Soul that no human can touch. You then have two hearts. One that pumps blood through your veins and one that pumps the love of God into your existence.

To God be the glory for the things He has done.

LUCIFER was an archangel. A leader of other angels in heaven. He started smelling himself and thought he could take over God's Kingdom. He and the other angels he convinced to follow him were kicked out of heaven. They landed on earth and have been raising sin ever since. The devil is for real. Scripture tells us how he tried to tempt Jesus after Jesus was baptized by John the Baptist. Satan went after Jesus and he will go after you. You do not go to church on Sunday because you want to. You go because in the back of your mind you know you need God. The devil will turn you inside out if it were not for Jesus. When you hear someone say the devil made me do it, believe it. Scripture tells us that Lucifer communicated directly with God. God told him that there was nothing he could do to destroy the faith of JOB. We often wonder why God permitted JOB to suffer as he did. We often wonder why God would permit Satan to continue his harmful ways. God wants you to need Him. God wants you to love, trust, and have faith in Him. Think about it. If you believed that you did not need God in your life, you would not be the person you are. You are not only doing it for God, you are also doing it for yourself.

Lucifer, Satan, devil, evil one whatever you want to call him is for real. He knows he has lost the war, but, he will not stop fighting. He wants to prevent every person he can from enjoying the Victory of Jesus. God is good. There is something that God cannot do. He cannot commit evil acts. Everything that is good come from God. Everything that is evil come from Satan. Stop believing that God brought sickness or pain upon you. Stop believing that floods, fire, and hurt came from God. The devil made these things happen. All tribulation comes from the devil. Our faith in God and being patient alone gives us the resilience to face the acts of the evil one and overcome. We must know our enemy. We must know his strong points and his weakness. We believe in God. We must also believe that our enemy, Satan, lives and will forever be a danger in our lives.

Lucifer has a major weakness, the Trinity. God, Jesus, the Holy Ghost.

Get It Right The First Time

Get It Right The First Time

Life is not a dress rehearsal. We have one chance to get it right. One life to live. We must make choices. We can only hope that they are the right choices. Some people have made the decision to follow God through His Son Jesus the Christ. Others have made the decision to follow God without Jesus. Some have made the decision not to follow God at all. We will never know in this life which choice was the right choice. It is a matter of faith. There are different degrees of faith. Some faith is stronger than others. Some faith is so strong that it will stand any test. It accepts the fact that winds will blow in our lives. It accepts the fact that we will get burned. But, that faith is so strong that it also believes the fire can never burn us up. This faith believes that no one and nothing can destroy our soul and spirit. Our faith in God, Jesus and the Holy Ghost will live with us forever. Forever includes after death. Our Souls and our Spirits will live forever. That is what Jesus told us when He said those who believe in God and Him will never die. Everlasting life through eternity. The right choice. We don't need to know during this life that our decision was right. Our love for God and Jesus can only be right. We have made some mistakes in our lives, but, the most important decision will be with us forever. Nothing, not even death, can separate us from our love of God through Jesus Christ. NOTHING.

Saved II

Must you believe in Jesus Christ to be SAVED? There are billions of people in this world who believe in God, but, not in Jesus. They are down on their hands and knees everyday praying to God. They live their lives in a God fearing manner. Are all of this people going to Hades? What about the people who are born into Communist controlled territories? They are forbidden to even speak the name of Jesus. They know nothing about Him. Will our JUST God commit them to Hades? We must the careful not to trend into God's territory. The fact is, we don't know and we are not suppose to know. You will have many Christians make statements, but, they are only stating their opinions. They believe in Jesus and they state that Jesus is the only way to God. Maybe they are right. But again, we must understand that we serve a just God. God will not punish those who have not had the opportunity to learn about Jesus. It is possible that God will turn His back on those who had the opportunity but rejected Jesus.

How were people SAVED before Jesus came into this world? Read the Old Testament closely and you will find that people thousands of years before the birth of Jesus knew of His coming. Abraham, Moses, Job all made statements telling everyone that the Messiah was coming. They were saved because they believed in the Messiah. They believed in their Saviour. God knew of the coming of Jesus into this world. God forgave the sins of righteous people because of the future contribution of Jesus. God forgave their sins because of their FAITH. Faith in the love of God. Faith that God would make a way somehow. Faith that the Messiah would make it possible for them to live for eternity with Him. Jesus was before the existence of this earth. God and Jesus, not God alone. People have always been saved by Jesus from Adam and Eve to now. Jesus has always been there doing God's work. Human beings are not a higher form of animal. We are God's form. We were made from His image. God gave us a heart and a soul that no human can see or touch. There are people who believe in Jesus who do not even know it. They are controlled by the Holy Spirit and don't even realize it is happening.

Must you believe in Jesus to be Saved? That's God's territory. But for me and my house, we will serve the Lord. Jesus is Lord. Praise His Holy Name.

God's Territory

The capacity of the human mind is without description. Rocket scientist. People who can develop means to carry man to the moon. Who can develop weapons capable of killing millions of people. Brain surgeons. Surgeons who can change a man into a woman. Or can they? Does man have his limitations? Wisdom. These limitations go beyond mental capacity. Surgery can change the appearance of a person, but, it can never change God's purpose. A transsexual male can never birth a child. God has placed limitations on the capacity of man. Man can do the extraordinary, but, God's limitations will not permit him to enter God's territory. We have been told not to conform to this world. We have been told to transform to the likeness of God.

We have heard that there is a difference between a transsexual and a homosexual. We have been told that a transsexual is who you are. A homosexual is who you love. People who believe this do not understand one important part of this equation. God. Who you are is a child of God. Who you love far-most is God. Almost all things are accessible, but, not all things are wise.

There is nothing earthly, other than the mind, that is materially more important to human beings than the body. The one thing humanity must learn is that God sees and passes judgement on what is inside of you. You can change your outward appearance all you want, but, you will never be able to change God's point of view. Once you realize and accept this, you will start to live your life in accordance to the directions of God. If He wanted you to be a female or male, He would have made you one. Stop trending into God's territory. If He wanted you to have sex with a male He would have made you a female. God's Will not yours. His Will does not stop your human desires. His Will controls your human desires. There are certain things you will not do because you know that God does not approve. You will not try to change your God given sexuality because you will not enter into the territory of God.

The capacity of the human mind is without description. God has placed His limitations even on the human mind. He has left one door open. That being the wisdom for man to know his limitation and never to enter into God's territory.

Judgement Day

The Lutheran Church was the first Protestant denomination. They believe that the only factor that will determine acceptance into heaven is the Grace of God. Not even faith plays a factor. The pure at heart will see God. The thief who died on a cross next to Jesus is an example. Jesus told the thief that he will be with Jesus in paradise. This tells us that a pure heart at the time of death is God's most important consideration. How you live your life is secondary to having a pure heart. God has told us that He will have mercy on whom He will have mercy. These truths however should not lead us to believe that our manner of living has no importance and will not be given consideration come judgement day. God gave us the Ten Commandments for a reason. Are we to believe that, come judgement day, God will completely disregard our efforts to obey His commands?

Jesus told us in the gospel of John that the time is coming when all who are in the grave will hear His voice and come out. Those who have DONE GOOD will rise to live and those who have done evil will rise to be condemned. Jesus also told us in the gospel of Matthew that the Son of Man is going to come in His Father's glory and will reward each person according to what HE HAS DONE. Scripture in Hebrews, Revelation, Jeremiah, and Romans tells us that we serve a Just God. He will not forget our efforts to help His people. He will not forget our efforts to live a life pleasing in His sight.

There might be some understanding where I fall short. But I am one who believes that God looks at the whole picture. I am one who believes that a pure heart is God's most important consideration. I am one who also believes that faith and obedience to His word are very valuable considerations. We serve a Just God. Trust in Jesus. He won't let you down.

Barriers

ISIS

Nothing in life just happens. The Muslim movement got its start long ago. Genesis 17 will tell the story of the start of this movement of hate. Abraham had his first son by his maidservant Hagar. The boy was given the name Ishamael. Hagar and her son Ishamael were put out of Abraham's household. Hagar was an Egyptian. As Ishamael grew, The Egyptian formed hate in his heart for all Jews. This hate continued from generation to generation. Muhammad because the leader of the Muslim movement. He demanded death of all Jews and Christians. The ISIS movement today is lead by Islamic terrorist who follow the teaching of Muhammad and who hate both Jews and Christians.

PROTESTANT DENOMINATION

Nothing in life just happens. In the 16th century, the Roman Catholic Church was in total control of the Christian movement. They believed that a person could be forgiven for sin by personal contributions. Martin Luther did not agree with this belief. Leaders of the Roman Catholic church tried to kill him. It was not his intention to start a denomination separate from that of the Catholic church, but, because of his efforts to change the Roman Catholic church the Lutheran church was formed. This movement was the beginning of the Protestant denomination. The Lutheran church believes that humans can do nothing to earn forgiveness for sin. They believe that not even faith plays a part in Salvation. Salvation can be granted only through the Grace of God. They believe the actions of humans have absolutely no effect.

Numerous other movements followed the establishment of the Lutheran church. They all, including the Catholic church, believe in Jesus Christ. They all have their minor differences, however, Jesus is the force that holds all of them together. Catholic and Protestants now worship together praising the name of Jesus. Both are Christians.

The above tells us that we cannot have the glory without the weight. We can't be blessed without obeying the government of God. It also tells us that life is like a puzzle and Jesus is the missing piece. We must fight through the evil ways of groups like ISIS. We must even fight through our own mistakes like those made by the early Roman Catholic church. God has been at work through history to break through barriers. We will not forget. The axle forgets early but the tree never forgets. Being a Christian is not easy. Many have died and continue today to die in their efforts to follow Jesus.

We Christians must remember that God will have the last word. Sometimes we have to go through troubles. Sometimes we wonder why there are so many pot holes in this road God has placed us on. Because of our love, trust and faith in God, we will stay on this road not knowing. We would not if we might. For it is better to walk in the darkness with God than to walk alone in the light. Our roads ahead will get rocky. But we will fight a good fight. We will stay the course. We will keep the faith. Faith that one day God will carry us to the Promised Land were we will have life with Him and with our Saviour Jesus forever.

I Don't Know, But

I Don't Know, But

There are some who believe that because Jesus died on the Cross all our sins have been forgiven. Jesus gave His blood for the purpose of taking away the past, present, and future sins of humanity. If we have accepted Jesus as our Savior, when we stand before the Lord Jesus on judgment day, our sins will not even be considered. That sounds wonderful. Then, It is difficult to understand why Jesus said that we will be judged on the good things and bad things we have done while in this body. There are some who believe that the suffering and death of Jesus will only wiped out our sins if we sincerely repent. Sincerely seek forgiveness from God. They believe that it takes more to be Saved than only saying Jesus is Lord and believing that God raised Him from the dead. It takes trying your best to live your life to the Glory of God. Jesus told Peter that he too would perish if he did not repent. You are a sinner. There is nothing you can do about it. You only have the one way out that Jesus gave you. Don't depend on your own understanding. Be sure to touch all the bases if you have hit what could be an inside the LIFE HOME run. Confess with your mouth that Jesus Christ is Lord. Believe in His Resurrection. Repent. Ask God to forgive you for your sins. Live your life in a manner that will please God. I don't know who is right or who is wrong. But, I do know that we serve a Just and Loving God. When we live for God, we can't go wrong.

Understanding II

Understanding II

Have you ever asked the Lord why there is so much suffering in this world? Have you ever asked God why bad things have to happen to good people? I have. He told me to shut-up. He told me that He did not owe me an explanation for anything. I am God all by Myself. It's My thing. I will do what I want to do. You don't understand, even know, My overall plan for earth. Stay in your place. I told you what to do and how to do it. Now make a decision. Either you will accept Me as I am for who I am or you will not. Stop playing games with Me. I am not going to force you to do anything. Force is only temporary. Know that I am God. Maker of heaven and earth. Know that I love you and will work everything out for your good. I have created this world for you to enjoy if you are wise enough to know where the enjoyment lies. I have given you a limited number of years to gain understanding of your life. I have given you a mind and heart to do so. Those who take advantage of this offering will benefit after your limited time in this life is complete. Know thee that I am God and that every living thing will eventually answer to Me. Live your life for Me and I will give you eternal blessings.

We Have A Pill For That

Pills don't cure the illness they only treat the symptoms. Often in life, we give in to treating the symptoms because we do not want to go through the pain necessary in addressing the cure. It hurts. So, we take a pain pill for temporary relief. Maybe we must suffer to have permanent relief. We often wonder why there is so much suffering in this world. Maybe we must suffer to show our love for God just as Jesus suffered to show His love for us. Sometimes we have to get out of our way. We have to make a determination that God is our priority. Sometimes this life takes a second place to God. We are weak. We need reinforcement to keep it all together. It has been said that a bible that is falling apart usually belongs to a person who is not. We read the bible not only for knowledge, but, for peace of mind. Go to church on Sunday and you will hear the name of Jesus twice as much as you hear the name God. We praise Jesus. We worship God. When we look at Jesus, we see God. Jesus was at the right hand of God before (They) created heaven and earth. The people who lived during the times the New Testament was enacted, during the earthly times of Jesus, had the Old Testament to refer to. Those of the Old Testament believed the Messiah was coming. There are numerous verses in the Old Testament telling of the coming of the Messiah. None more detailed than that of Isaiah. Isaiah was a prophet, poet, and politician who out lived four kings. He warned many kings of the danger of relying on military power and wealth more than relying on God. Chapter 53 in Isaiah tells in detail of the coming of Jesus. Jesus was sent to us to address the cure not, like a pill, to temporary relieve the pain. Jesus was sent to us to tell us of the Grace of God. Nothing is more important than the Grace of God. Only by His Grace will we receive Eternal Life. Nothing should be more important to us than receiving Eternal Life. Some of us will die at age six. Some at age eighty. But, die we will. Or will we? For he who believes in Jesus will never die. You will leave this earth, but, you will never die. The greatest blessing. To live with God and His Son Jesus FOREVER.

Researchers have stated that a human being has between five and nine senses. Use one of them to prove that there is a God. You want there to be a God. That is the reason you believe in Him. You know that you have very little control in this life and absolutely none thereafter. All you have is HOPE. Hope that there is a Creator of heaven and earth. Hope that He loves you. Hope that He will make everything alright. Without hope this life would not be worth living. You are a Christian. You believe in God, Jesus, and the Holy Ghost.

Without hope, you would turn into a Humanist. You would be a member of the Humanism religion. You would be a person who has given up on this life. You would believe that there is no God. That God is nothing more than a product of man's imagination. Humanist religion defies man and rejects God. Deny that man has a Soul. Man is not a sinner and does not need another Force to solve his problems. There is no eternality. This universe created itself thus Humanism is based on individual worth and rationalism. Man is the supreme authority, therefore, there is no eternal destiny.

Christians can only pray for Humanist. All the reason and rationalism in this world can never make me not believe in God. Yet, too many Christians live like Humanist. They are called weak hearted Christians. There is a difference between a weak heart and a strong heart Christian. A weak heart Christian does believe in God, Jesus, and the Holy Ghost, but, will not turn his/her life over to God. Will not take anything that does not belong to them as long as they do not know who it belongs to. Will not hurt anyone if it is happening before his eyes. Continues to have sex with a member of their own gender stating that God wants us to love one another. Continues to use drugs stating that he is not hurting anyone else. A weak heart Christian will always find logic to do what he wants to do and not do what God wants him to do. No, he is not a Humanist, but, he is not yet a true Christian.

Does God control your life? Total control? This can be true only when nothing on the face of this earth is more important to you than God. You might have to walk through Hades, but, you will still have God. Live your life for God. That's what He wants. God does not want to be a choice when an important decision has to be made. There is only one way. God's Way. Show Him and this world that you live for God and God alone.

Jesus

Christians believe in Jesus. Most Christians do not understand the Divine Nature of Jesus. Jesus was not created by God. God formed Jesus after His own image to do God's work. Jesus is the body of God Almighty. The mind and body of Jesus is God. The bible states that God said (let US create man after Our own image). The words US and OUR tell us that someone was there with God. That someone was Jesus. Jesus was with God far before the creation of heaven and earth. The question has been asked, how were people Saved before Jesus? There were no people before Jesus. Jesus has always been at the right hand of God doing the work of God. The Old Testament was written thousands of years before the New Testament. Yet, the people of the Old Testament believed that God would send a Messiah to save the world. The Book of Isaiah states that a Messiah is coming from Galilee. Micah lived 500 years before the birth of Jesus into this world. Yet, he stated clearly that the Messiah would be born in Bethlehem and that He will be King of Kings and Lord of Lords.

We Christians of today must understand who Jesus really is. We must turn our backs on any words that lessen the Divine Nature of Jesus the Christ. God gave us Jesus because He knew that we, being human, needed someone close to believe in. Someone who has walked this earth and been seen and touched by the human hand. God, before Jesus, sent many prophets to tell His word. Too often His word fell on deaf ears. Because of the limitations of men, God sent His Son. The Word became flesh and made His dwelling among us. No one has ever seen God, but, Jesus who has always been at the Father's side, has made Him known.

It's time to live the life you sing about in your song. Jesus is Lord. The Lord has been good to me. Jesus is the best thing that has ever happened to me.

Heaven

Our primary goal. Nothing is more important than going to heaven. We are all going to die, but, life would be a terrible experience if we did not believe that there was something better waiting for us. After all, what good is working for something that you know you are going to lose anyway? Life has to have some meaning more that just here and now. We might even be afraid of death because we don't know how it will all play out. We believe in something we cannot see or touch, our Souls. We believe in God whom we cannot see or touch. We only have faith. That which we hope for and are certain of. We can't see or touch faith, but, we know we have it. Faith in our Heavenly Father. Faith that He will make everything alright. Without faith, we have no life. We believe that we must please God in this life to have an opportunity to get to heaven. Without faith, it is impossible to please God.

There are some religious denominations that believe faith has no bearing on getting to heaven. They believe that only the Grace of God will make that determination. If this is true, then what value is FAITH? Jesus gave Bartimaeus his sight. Jesus said to him your faith has healed you. There was a needy woman who touched the hem of the garment of Jesus. Jesus said to her your faith has made you whole. What value if FAITH? Faith reveals the presence of God in our lives. God wants you to live your life more abundantly. By faith you will. Faith, permits us to believe that God does exist and will reward us in our efforts to live a life that is pleasing in His sight. This life is worth living because of our faith in God.

Grace is God's. Faith is Yours.

Paid In Full

During the Christmas season my kids come by and we exchange gifts. Then they go home to enjoy Christmas day with their families. I normally spend Christmas Day by myself. One Christmas Day I went to Steak & Shake to get something to eat. There was a white lady in her sixties who I could feel was looking at me. When I looked her way, she continued to eat her food. When I looked up again, she was gone. I finished my food and asked the waiter for the bill. He told me that my ticket had been paid in full. I do not know why that lady decided to bless me. I had never seen her before and I would not know her if I saw her again. I do not know why Jesus decided to bless me. He didn't have to do it. He didn't have to go through such pain for me. Nails in His wrist and feet. Sword driven into His side. Why? Love. Love of His Father and love for all of humanity. He washed away our sins. And now, unto Him who is able to keep you from falling and present you faultless before His glories presents. We so often think of how we have lived our lives. We mentally punish ourselves for the wrongs that we have done and for that which we should have done but did not. Stop! Know that you are human and that you will sin. Know that Jesus paid the price for our sins of the past, present, and future. We have only to do right and be right. By doing so, we pay Jesus gratitude.

I once worked for a car rental company. One November day I decided to stop at a truck stop to eat lunch. This truck stop had good fresh salads for only $2.99. I made my selection and started to the cashier. A young black man, six feet tall and in his twenties, took the salad out of my hands and told me to put my money away. I had never seen him before. I tried to tell him that I could make the payment. He gave the cashier full payment. He said Merry Christmas. Then he disappeared. Why me? Why did he pick me to bless? When the Holy Spirit is within you, it makes you do things without thinking. It does not matter what you look like. The Holy Spirit is within. The Holy Spirit was within Jesus. He knew that His sacrifice would bless the world.

We should be living life in the beauty of holiness. Jesus has paid the price in full. It is finished. We only have to accept His blessings and praise His Holy Name.

Printed in the United States
By Bookmasters